Miracles

ASK AND YE SHALL RECEIVE

© MICHAEL R. BINDER, M.D.
Resurrection Sunday
April 24th, 2011

ISBN: 978-0-9748836-3-2

AUTHOR'S PREFACE

I first thought to write this book about fifteen years ago, but every time I penned one miracle, three more came to mind. After ten minutes of writing, I recalled so many miracles that I realized I had far too little time to get them all down on paper, let alone organize them into a book. So I shelved the project. But thanks to this latest miracle, I finally found the time.

Before going any further, I would like to define what I mean by "miracle." My definition of a miracle is an experience that demonstrates God's providence to the individual. Hence, miracles are not limited to those rare dramatic events that cannot be explained in the natural but include those personal experiences, however common or seemingly insignificant, that demonstrate the presence of God to a person. For instance, if someone applied for a job, went through the interview process, and was hired, most of us would not think that anything miraculous happened. However, the person who got the job might see things differently. Perhaps he or she had been hopelessly unable to find a job until turning to God for help. Or perhaps the job offer came on the heels of an act of faith that in the natural should have worked against being hired, such as an honest disclosure of a personal short-coming or conflicting interest. Notwithstanding, most, if not all, of the miracles I have recorded in this book do defy the odds. I chose them in the hope that they would deepen the reader's faith in God, as they have mine.

This book contains just some of the miracles I have experienced. There are some that I did not recall as of the writing of this book, and still others that I cannot share because they involve confidential patient care. I should also point out that not every prayer was answered immediately. There have been times when I have had to wait, but the waiting was well-worth the effort because God answered many of my prayers in ways far beyond what I had ever hoped or imagined. But whether the wait was long or short, one thing is clear: there has never been a prayer that I have offered with faith that has not been answered. And that is the greatest miracle of all!

May this book be a miracle in the life of every person who reads it. Amen.

To my mother and my grandmother,
who taught me to have faith;

To my Lord,
who empowered me to have faith;

To my readers,
with whom I share my faith.

TABLE OF CONTENTS

CHAPTER 1
MIRACLES DURING MY CHILDHOOD

CHAPTER 2
MIRACLES DURING MY ADOLESCENCE

CHAPTER 3
MIRACLES DURING MY COLLEGE YEARS

CHAPTER 4
MIRACLES DURING MEDICAL SCHOOL AND RESIDENCY

CHAPTER 5
MIRACLES IN MY FAMILY LIFE

CHAPTER 6

MIRACLES IN MY PROFESSIONAL LIFE

CHAPTER 7

MIRACLES IN MY PERSONAL LIFE

There are two ways to live your life One is as though nothing is a miracle. The other is as though everything is a miracle.

ALBERT EINSTEIN

Behold, I stand at the door, and knock: if any man hear my voice, and open the door, I will come in to him, and will sup with him, and he with me. Rev. 3:20, KJV.

"And all things, whatsoever ye shall ask in prayer, believing, ye shall receive."

—The Son of God

✝

CHAPTER 1

—⟨⟨∗⟩⟩—

MIRACLES DURING MY CHILDHOOD

Called to the Window

When I was about four years old, we lived a few blocks from my grandmother's house. One day I took my little sister by the hand and walked down the street from our house to my grandmother's. I don't remember the reason for doing it, but I do remember feeling desperate enough to do such a daring thing. When we arrived at the three-story apartment building in which my grandparents lived, we were too young to understand how to enter through the lobby. Yet just as I started wondering what to do, my grandmother called down to us from the second floor window.

It was not until nearly fifty years later that my grandmother and I got to talking about that day, and I thought to ask her how she knew to come to the window when my sister and I had arrived downstairs.

She said she was in another room in the apartment, and for no logical reason, something told her to go to the living room window. She said she thought it strange because she rarely ever looked out that window. But when she obeyed the voice, there my sister and I were, holding hands in front of the building, trying to figure out how to let her know we were there.

Some people might interpret this as a lucky coincidence, but the timing was so precise that neither my grandmother nor I have any doubt that the Holy Spirit had called her to the window.

Two Miracles on the Beach

As I was growing up, I spent most of my summers on the beach because my mother loved laying in the sun. So I would build sandcastles, catch Minnows, and chase butterflies. There on the beach I even taught myself to swim.

One day, I was getting very bored on the beach and saw people playing frisbee. Though my mother was always there to give my sister and me a listening ear and an example of faith, she rarely bought us toys. So on that particular day, I started to pray for a Frisbee. I gave no thought to how or where I was going to get one; I just remember wishing for one. About twenty minutes later, I accidentally uncovered a large, brand-new, black and silver Frisbee! In all the years I had spent on the beach digging around in the sand, I had never found anything like that. As I look back on that day, there is no doubt in my mind that God had answered my prayer.

On another occasion, my mother made an unusual suggestion. She told me to stop chasing the butterflies lest they fly off and warn the others to stay away from the beach. Her suggestion did not make much sense to me because on that day, like most others, there were very few butterflies around to begin with, and I could not understand how ignoring the few that I did see was going to help me catch one of them!

Nevertheless, I did what she said. Within an hour, I began to see increasing numbers of Monarch butterflies on the beach. As the hours passed, there were more and more. Eventually, they were everywhere!!! There were literally thousands of them swarming the beach. Most of them were landing on the sand and hardly moving, which of course allowed me to catch them with ease. I was catching them left and right, holding them between my fingers, three or four in each hand. I took home as many as I could fit into an empty jar of cold cream that my mother had given me. Though I did not fully understand it at the time, I can now see that God was beginning to teach me the value of obedience. He had clued my mother in to something that she normally would not have known—that the Monarchs were migrating—and used it to teach me one of the most valuable disciplines we can learn.

The Power of the Spirit

When I was in second grade, I was a few minutes late for school one day and experienced something I will never forget. When I walked into the coatroom, which was separated from the classroom by a dividing wall, I was jumped from behind by two of my classmates, who started punching and kicking me. The whole thing was so frightening and unexpected that all I could do was bend down and try to protect myself. In the process, my shirt was partially torn off, and I continued to feel completely helpless until I saw that they had broken the chain of my cross. Suddenly, I found myself become a fearless defender of the faith. Filled with righteous indignation over what they had done to the precious symbol of God, I abruptly straightened up and with a thundering voice and fiery eyes said, "You broke my chain!" At that, they abruptly stopped punching me and ran out of the coatroom. Of course, the teacher then became aware that something had happened. Moments later, she came into the coatroom to find that I had been assaulted.

After the other two boys had been questioned, I was told by the principal that they had mistaken me for another boy against whom they were retaliating. The boys never apologized to me but neither did they ever bother me again.

For me, the miracle was not so much that they never bothered me again but rather the dramatic change in my demeanor the moment I saw that they had broken my cross. Without any thought, I went from helpless victim to staunch defender of the faith. That's the power of the Holy Spirit!

Miracle of the Shark's Tooth

Every winter when I was a boy, we would travel south to the sunny, warm water beaches of Florida or South Carolina. One particular trip was unforgettable.

When we arrived in Myrtle Beach that winter, I met some children who were collecting little black shells along the seashore. When I asked if I could see one of them, the little girl opened her hand to show me her prized possession—a tiny shark's tooth about the size of a watermelon seed.

It seemed that everyone on the beach was looking for them. Then I noticed that the girl's father was proudly wearing a much larger one on his neck-chain. I was amazed at the size and asked him where he had gotten it. He told me he had been vacationing in South Carolina for over twenty years and that the one he was wearing was the largest he had ever found.

I had seen and heard enough. I decided to spend my entire vacation looking for shark's teeth. I began my search immediately, but had no luck. After several walks up and down the beach, I began to realize that finding a shark's tooth was not going to be an easy task. Hour after hour I walked along the beach scarcely taking my eyes off the shore in hopes of finding one of those precious teeth. Gradually, the hours turned into days, and still no shark's tooth.

After nearly a week of searching, the final day of our trip had arrived. Once again, I spent the entire time searching for shark's teeth, but again found nothing. At last, the time for us to leave had arrived. Seeing that I remained determined to find a shark's tooth, my mother allowed me to take one last walk up the beach. Hurriedly, I continued my search, but again had no luck. Feeling completely discouraged, I paused for a moment, only to see my mother and sister shaking sand off their towels in preparation to return to the hotel. In desperation, I looked up to the heavens and said, "O God, I have tried everything; please help me find a shark's tooth." I had scarcely finished my prayer when I received the thought that exactly one-hundred yards down the beach a shark's tooth would be waiting for me. Uncertain of what to make of this, I looked down the shoreline approximately the length of a football field. That was very close to where my family was gathering our things in preparation to leave. With that, I debated whether to stop my search and walk directly to the area one hundred yards ahead, or continue my search as I walked toward that point. This was a crucial decision, as I feared that the tooth might wash back into the water if I did not arrive at the right place at the right time. Then again, if the tooth were not there, I would be out of luck because it was time to go. In an effort not to lose ground, I decided to continue my search but with the caveat that I would pay extra close attention when I reached the area one-hundred yards ahead. As I resumed my hurried but methodical search, I was reminded of the importance of faith in prayer. I thought about that for a moment and again considered the option of proceeding directly to the target area. On a practical level, I wanted to keep my eyes focused on the shoreline so as not to forfeit my last opportunity to find a shark's tooth; but on a spiritual level, I wanted to demonstrate my trust in God.

In a giant leap of faith, I decided to peel my eyes off the shoreline and proceed directly to the point one hundred yards ahead. As I carefully stepped off the distance, my hope of finding a shark's tooth was challenged by the thought that I was throwing away my last chance to find one. Nevertheless, I felt that this approach would demonstrate the integrity of my faith while at the same time ensuring that I arrived at the right place at the right time. Oh how difficult it was to place all my trust in the invisible God.

When I reached the point one hundred yards ahead, I quickly dashed my eyes back down to the shoreline in high hopes of finding the shark's tooth that had been promised me. To my chagrin, I saw nothing but a big black rock chasing a wave back into the water. There was nothing else in sight.

Realizing that my search and my vacation had come to an abrupt end, I again reached for the faith that had led me to that point and halfheartedly chased after the black rock that I saw tumbling back into the water. I caught up with it just as it disappeared under the surf. Trying not to lose faith, I plunged my hand into the foamy water and felt around for the rock. As I lifted my hand out of the water and brought it close to my face, a clump of wet sand and tiny shells sifted through my fingers to expose the very same rock that I saw tumbling into the water. In sadness, I stared at it, trying not to lose hope. As I tried to gather myself, I began to notice that this was not an ordinary rock. It was triangular shaped with serrated edges that came to a point opposite its base. Suddenly, I realized that this was not a rock at all—it was a giant shark's tooth!!! Overwhelmed with excitement, I hurried to show my mother. She shared in my excitement and offered to take me to an area store to have it mounted on a neck-chain.

When I arrived at the store, the attendant was so impressed by the tooth that he asked to buy it from me. I graciously declined, but the offer reaffirmed the wonder of the miracle. I proudly wore that shark's tooth on a neck-chain for many years. Eventually, the mounting wire broke, and my grandmother gave me a cross to wear instead. The last place I recall seeing the tooth was in the drawer of the desk in my room when I was in high school.

I have shared this inspiring story with many people over the years, and I have often been asked if I still have the tooth. Unfortunately, I have always had to tell people that it was lost in a move while I was away at college.

Then one day I got to thinking: with all the people who have asked to see the shark's tooth, I should seriously investigate what happened to it. I began by asking my grandmother (with whom I had been living before I left for college) to look through her jewelry for the tooth. When she couldn't find it, I took another look through all my things. When that was unsuccessful, I said a halfhearted prayer asking God to help me find the tooth.

A year passed, and I was still no closer to finding the long-lost shark's tooth. Meanwhile, more and more people who heard the story wanted to see the tooth. So I became absolutely determined to find it. I started to ask my grandmother ridiculous questions like, who bought the house that was sold thirty years ago? and where did my desk go? Needless to say, nobody could remember. Not only that, my family was laughing at the ridiculousness of the investigation. So I turned to God and repeated the prayer to find the tooth, this time in earnest; I mean I really prayed, just like I had that day I found the tooth on the beach.

A few weeks later, someone stopped into my office with a package. She told me that she had been helping her parents move and that something had told her that this item she brought me would be best in my care.

When I looked inside the bag, I was shocked to find an enormous tooth! I initially thought it was a shark's tooth, but it was actually a whale's tooth!!! It was the size of a large candle and looked completely natural, as though it had been found on the beach.

Then I noticed something that went straight to my heart. Carved into the rock-hard ivory on the reverse side of the tooth was the body of Jesus Christ hanging on the cross. The workmanship was no less amazing than the fact that the person who had brought it to me knew nothing about the lost tooth or my prayer. The whole thing was even more miraculous than finding the long-lost tooth would have been. Beyond that, this was an autographed version, signed by God Himself. He sent it to me as if to say, If you had any doubt about who led you to that tooth when you were a little boy, it was Me, Jesus. And there He was, hanging on the cross as a demonstration of His infinite love for all of us.

I continue to tell this story (and show the tooth) to all those who are interested. It is not only visual proof of God's providence and desire to have an intimate relationship with us but it is also proof that Jesus Christ and God are one in the same.

+ + +

✝

CHAPTER 2

—⚬❧✝❧⚬—

MIRACLES DURING MY ADOLESCENCE

Field of Dreams

As I was growing up, my favorite sport was baseball. But I was raised in a single-parent home that had its advantages and disadvantages. On the one hand, it gave me lots of freedom, but on the other, that freedom was largely unsupervised. Since we lived in a part of the city that was quite a distance from any park, there was not much opportunity to play baseball on a field much less in an organized baseball league. Consequently, allies and empty parking lots were our baseball fields, sticks and stones were our bases, and porches and fences were our home-run walls.

By the time I had reached fifth or sixth grade, I was getting more creative and ambitious. So I decided to organize a baseball league for my friends and me. I made a roster of players and designated a distant park that I had discovered as our new playing field. With the help of a family friend, I had it all typed out and made official. Then I handed out copies to my friends in the neighborhood. After all that work, I can remember us playing about three innings before it all fell apart.

Some time after that, I came up with another idea. I had somehow learned that there was a park in the community that hosted a Little League baseball program. So I found out when tryouts were and told my friends about it. I then convinced them to talk to their parents about the idea of carpooling because the park was so far away. Eventually, we got a couple of parents to buy into it and before I knew it, I was getting rides with my friends to tryouts.

After three or four practices, we were told that a notice would be posted in the clubhouse listing the names of the players who had made the team. To this day, I can remember all of us going to the park to see which of us had been chosen. As it turned out, all my friends had made it except for me. As I stood there trying to except the heartbreaking news, one of my friends noticed my name printed on another list—I had been chosen by a different team. This was quite unexpected because none of us had been trying out for that team, yet I was somehow picked by them. Though relieved, I faced a big problem because I would then have to find my own ride to most of my games.

Unfortunately, I was unable to find a ride, and so it did not work out for me. Ironically, I wound up playing very little baseball that summer because all my friends were getting their fill in the organized league I had found. Worse yet, I had nothing to do while all my friends were away at games and practices three nights a week. It left me with a lot of time to think about how much fun they were having.

At the end of the season, I learned that one of my close friends, Kelly Davis, had been selected as the league's most valuable player. He was awarded a large trophy, which he invited me to see at his home. It was really impressive.

Some time late that summer, Kelly and I decided to hike to a park with a baseball diamond for a one-on-one baseball game. Imagine that: just two players—a batter and a pitcher—chasing balls into the field and the batter around the bases for nine complete innings. In a very close game, I managed to defeat Kelly by one run. I will never forget his words to me after the game. He said, "You beat me fair and square. That trophy I won should belong to you." His comment made me feel as if I had just been named the league's most valuable player! Through my friend Kelly, my Father in Heaven reminded me that I had not been forgotten.

But the good Lord was not done yet. I believe it was the following summer that I was walking through the Sears Roebuck department store with my friend Steve when I saw two athletic-looking men walking in our direction. After they passed us, I said to Steve, "You know, I think those guys are professional athletes." He asked me how I knew that because both of them were dressed in indistinct clothing. I told him I didn't know; I just had a feeling. And so I quickly ran past them, turned around, and started walking toward them again. As we approached each other, I stopped and asked, "Excuse me, are you guys professional athletes?" They paused for a moment and smiled. Then one of them said, "We play for the Chicago Cubs."

By that time, my friend Steve had caught up with us, at which point the two men asked if we would like to come to the game the following day. Of course, we accepted with glee! Then one of them pulled a little notebook out of his shirt pocket and wrote down our names. He told us our admission tickets would be waiting for us at the Box Office.

So the next day, Steve and I headed for Wrigley Field. I can remember being so little that I could barely see over the edge of the Box Office counter. And at that point, Steve and I still had no proof that the whole thing was for real. But the moment I gave the attendant my name, he plopped our tickets down on the counter. Steve and I couldn't believe it. We went in and found our seats in the fourth row over the Cubs dugout!

I will never forget that beautiful day. What I remember most was coming to the top of the stairwell to Wrigley Field and suddenly being struck by a gentle breeze as I beheld for the first time that immaculate field. I distinctly remember the sun shining down and brightly coloring the freshly mowed grass and pristine white bases with flags flying high and seats being filled with excited fans. As I continued to look on, my eyes fell upon right field, and I spontaneously uttered this prayer to God: "Lord, please let me play on this field one day." Thanks to the kindness and generosity of Chicago Cubs players Bill Madlock and Andy Thornton, I had seen a professional baseball field for the first time.

The magic continues…

After I graduated from grammar school, we moved to a new school district where there was a neighborhood park called Pottawattomie. I soon learned that "Pott" hosted an organized baseball league. I can remember walking across the park on my way home from school one day and casting a wish that I would play lots of baseball there. I really needed the experience because I had been planning to try out for the high school baseball team.

So I signed up for Pony League baseball in my age group. I also found a resourceful way to play with the older guys in Colt League. After my Pony League games, I would change out of my uniform and into neutral sweats. Then I would hang around the Colt League dugouts playing catch and looking for an opportunity to fill in if one team or the other were short a player. More often than not, I would get a chance to play! That summer I was playing baseball an average of six hours a day and building a lot of confidence.

In one of the last Colt League games of the season, I squeezed into the lineup and became the star player by making a saving catch and

9

knocking in the game-winning hit. As I was gathering my equipment after the game, a man who I had never met before was standing behind the fence waiting for me. As I walked toward him under the hum of the bright lights and smoke of the settling dust, I had the sense that he was some kind of baseball scout who wanted to talk to me about my ability. My intuition was right. First he asked me if I went to Sullivan High School, and then he asked me my name and told me that he was the assistant coach of the Varsity baseball team at my school. He asked me if I would be interested in playing in their summer league program. This was a golden opportunity for me—something I had never dreamt possible given that I was only a freshman in a new school and felt that my ability was far below the level of the Varsity players. So I became flooded with emotion as I imagined myself playing with a group of guys who at the time were bigger than life to me. Coach Pildes told me where and when they were playing their next game, and I told him I would be there.

I was so excited about the opportunity to play on the Varsity team that I arrived at the park an hour early. As I was loosening up, I watched in awe as one player after another arrived in his brightly colored uniform. Of course, they all knew one another, and here I was, all by myself, not even having a uniform. It was so intimidating.

As more and more players arrived, I began to fear that I was not going to get a chance to play. I knew that my only hope was that the team would be short a player, which would force them to use me, just as it had in the Colt League games. But as game time approached, we already had the required minimum of nine players, and I knew that more were on their way. For a while, no one else had arrived. But just as I started to get my hopes up, two more players got out of their car with a load of equipment. I thought to myself, that's it, now I will never get a chance to play.

As these last two guys approached the dugout, coach Pildes hollered out, "That's it, I'm sick of you two guys being late all the time; Binder is going to play!" I couldn't believe my ears—I was actually going to play!

In my first at bat, I followed Casey Robinson, the biggest jock at our school. As I was waiting on deck, I watched Casey pound a line drive to the center fielder. It was really impressive. As I took my turn in the batter's box, I thought to myself, how can I follow that? Feeling rather intimidated, I asked for a momentary time-out and stepped away from the plate to gather myself. Then I started thinking, if he can do it, I can do it. With that, I stepped back up to the plate and pounded a line drive right at the same fielder Casey hit his ball to. I don't think that center-fielder took more than a step to catch either ball. After that, I was convinced that I could play with those guys.

In my second year of high school, our team made the playoffs at Comiskey Park (now U.S. Cellular Field), but I was not a starter that year. However, the following year, we again made the playoffs, this time at Wrigley Field. I was the starting right-fielder that year. As I took my position in the outfield on the day of the game, I realized that my prayer had been answered. Not only that, I was standing right where I had been looking ten years earlier when, from the top of the stairwell, I had asked God to let me play on that field.

My high school baseball team in the Chicago Cubs dugout at Wrigley Field in the late innings of a semi-final city championship game. I am standing on the far left.

The Pain of Pride

The year after our trip to Wrigley Field, six of the nine players in our starting lineup, including me, had become high school seniors. Not surprisingly, our team that year was even better than the previous year. But little did we know, we had one thing working against us: we were cocky and competitive, even with one another. We were ruled more by a spirit of pride than unity, and I was no exception.

After an undefeated season that year, only one playoff game stood between us and a return to Wrigley Field. As I was loosening up in the outfield minutes before game time, the principal of the school we were playing came to wish me and my team good luck. I immediately recognized him as the former principal of the grammar school I had graduated from four years earlier. Perhaps because I was so keyed up and focused on the time, I did not pay much attention to the sentimentality of his visit and facetiously told him that his players had been wasting their time because there was no way they were going to win. His humble reply was, "Well, you never know." As he walked away, something about the way he said it gave me the feeling that I had said the wrong thing.

As expected, we took a big lead in the game. By the top half of the last inning, we had opened up a four-run lead and were again rallying with the bases loaded and nobody out when a line drive hit to right field was deemed a fair catch even though it appeared to have fallen in for a hit. The unfortunate result was an easy triple play. So although we still took the field with a four-run lead, the enormous shift in momentum suddenly made us feel as though we were behind in the game!

Then our ace pitcher, probably because he, like the rest of us, was so unnerved by the bad call, proceeded to walk one better after another. Unfortunately, a pitching change was not made until the winning run had come to the plate, but by then it was too late. Suddenly, all our hopes for a state championship and a return to Wrigley Field were dashed. The pain of it all haunts me to this day. But it was a powerful testimony to the danger of pride and of God's promise to confront it.

Love Reigns Supreme

Baseball was not the only sport I played at the organized level as I was growing up. I also played football, basketball, and hockey, and there were many exciting moments besides the trip to Wrigley Field. For instance, I also had the opportunity to play junior football at Soldier's Field and will never forget hearing my name called over the loudspeaker after I sacked the quarterback. But whether it was a big tackle, a great goal, or a game-winning hit, there was no sense of victory like that achieved by acts of love and character on the playing field. There were two instances in particular in which love reigned supreme. The first occurred in a post-season game in which we were trailing eleven to nothing; it was a game that was on the verge of being a no-hitter for the opposing pitcher. In the last inning with only two outs separating him from an achievement that is a true rarity in all of sports, I was one of the two last batters he had to face. As I settled into the batter's box, I remember feeling conflicted. On the one hand, doing my best to get a hit was the natural and expected thing for me to do; but on the other hand, it was clearly not worth depriving the pitcher of a memory that would last him a lifetime. Throwing a no-hitter would be an achievement that he could use to bolster his confidence in whatever trying situation he might find himself in later in life. With that in mind, I decided that I would intentionally strike out. But just as I made that decision, another thought came to mind. Was that really what he wanted me to do? I asked myself. So I motioned to the umpire for a brief time out. As I took a few practice swings outside the batter's box, I decided that it would be better to give him a chance to earn a real no-hitter. Suddenly, I found myself in a no-lose situation; to get a hit would be great, and to make an out would be no less great. With that, I stepped back into the batter's box with the intention of doing my best to get a hit. I will never forget the tremendous sense of wholeness and peace that I felt as I calmly waited for him to deliver his first pitch. He threw that first pitch right down the middle, and with sheer grace I pounded it into the gap in right-center field for a stand-up double. If there was any consolation, it was that the hit was neither lucky or cheap. In fact, it was the best stroke I can remember putting on a baseball! As I cruised into second base, I enjoyed the deep satisfaction of seeing my good-will efforts returned to me. I also congratulated the pitcher for what was still a remarkable achievement. And that's how it goes in life—we reap what we sow.

Some people would say that the attitude I took is contrary to healthy athletic competition. But on that day I learned that it is just the contrary; it brings athletic competition to true perfection. The magic of the story is that an act of love was even possible on the athletic field and yielded the same results that it does in every other aspect of life—it does even more for the giver than it does for the receiver.

The second victory of the human spirit occurred on a separate occasion in which our team suffered a narrow defeat. After the final out, the two teams formed lines to shake hands with their opponents, a formality that is still practiced in many sports. As I was congratulating each member of the winning team, I was thinking to myself, I should be happy for these guys seeing that they have won, just as I would have wanted them to be happy for us had we won. So I congratulated each player with a warm handshake and true happiness for him.

Afterward, I returned with my teammates to our own dugout. As we were gathering our equipment, a member of the other team walked into our dugout, approached me, and said, "You were truly happy for us, weren't you?" He then walked back to his dugout.

Although this might not sound like a very miraculous thing, anyone who has played competitive sports can attest to the dangerousness of coming on to the losing team's turf after they have just spent the last several hours trying to beat the crap out of you in every way possible—and failed!

So the miracle of the story is that this guy felt so moved by the goodwill that had been extended to him that he forgot himself enough to return the favor even at risk to himself. Far greater than any athletic victory, that was a victory of the human spirit!

A Blessing in Disguise

During the summer after high school graduation, I had been working for the park district as a little league baseball umpire. Toward the end of the season, there was a close play at first base in which I called the runner out. Well the player disagreed with my call and flew into a rage. As most umpires do, I stood calmly as the player jumped up and down in my face voicing his disagreement with the call. After a few moments, I told him that he needed to calm down. When he would not stop, I warned him that if he did not calm down and return to his dugout, I was going to eject him from the game. I then proceeded to walk from first base, where I had made the call, to the hitting area, where I bent for a moment to dust off home plate. When I stood back up, the kid was still in my face hollering at me. So I acted on my warning and threw him out of the game.

As he left the field, his coach came flying out of the dugout and started hollering at me the same way his player had been. Again, I calmly listened for awhile, but when he did not stop, I told him he was setting a poor example of sportsmanship for his team. Nonetheless, he continued to holler at me. At that point, I warned him that if he did not stop, I was going to throw him out of the game too.

Well, he kept right on, and so I followed through and ejected him from the game. With that, he walked off the field and stood behind the fence, alongside the player I had ejected. When play resumed, his team was left to fend for themselves without a coach. It was quite a sorry sight, but I felt justified in what I had done.

A few days later, I went into the clubhouse to pick up the schedule of upcoming games that I was assigned to umpire. To my surprise, my box was empty. In my confusion, I asked one of the other umpires what was going on. His response was, "Oh Mike, didn't you know? The coach you threw out of the game last week runs this program." I thought to myself, oops. So I thought about going and talking to him about it, but I decided that the job was not worth compromising my integrity.

Seeing that I still had three weeks left before my departure to California for the start of classes at UCLA, I sought and found a job at a new fast-food restaurant down the street from my house. About a week after I started, two guys pulled up to the restaurant on a motorcycle, came in, and placed their order. As I was serving them, I fell in love with the motorcycle they were riding. So I started thinking about how perfect it would be for me in California. As the thought of buying it from them crossed my mind, I had the hope that with winter in Chicago on its way, they might be willing to sell it.

So while they were sitting down waiting for their order, I approached them with an offer to buy the bike. Fortunately, the guy was interested. So I made him an offer, and we made arrangements to meet in front of my house after I had finished work.

When I returned to the cooking area, I was so excited about the prospect of buying the motorcycle that I absentmindedly burned all the food I was cooking. I will never forget seeing the customers lining up to return their over-cooked fish chips! All the while, I kept praying that the guy would follow through and show up at my house after work.

Well sure enough, at around four o'clock in the afternoon, the guy drove up with his motorcycle. After I had a chance to look it over, we settled on a price, and I gave him the cash.

The purchase of that motorcycle turned out to be even more important than I had thought at the time because I wound up residing with a family that lived deep in the Bel-Air canyon two miles from the university, and no public transportation was available. As it turned out, I boxed the motorcycle in a crate and shipped it to Los Angeles a week ahead of my departure so that it would be there waiting for me when I arrived. I wound up driving that motorcycle around L.A. during my first few years of college. It allowed me to get to and from school, it made parking possible in a city where there was virtually none, and it cost me only a couple dollars per month in gas!

I could never have known it at the time, but the loss of my job as an umpire played a crucial role in preparing me for college. It put me in position to see and purchase the motorcycle, a transportation vehicle that had been the furthest thing from my mind until I saw those two guys drive up with it when I was working at the restaurant. It was a demonstration of how integrity can close one door but open a bigger one!

+ + +

✝

CHAPTER 3

—⚬⚬⚬✝⚬⚬⚬—

MIRACLES DURING MY COLLEGE YEARS

A Special Meeting

By my senior year in high school, I was thinking seriously about becoming a doctor, but I found myself unable to decide whether to play baseball in college or fully devote myself to premedical studies. So I decided to apply to universities that would keep both doors open for me. I applied to Pacific Coast Conference schools like UCLA, USC, and Arizona State. I chose UCLA because I knew the tuition would be affordable once I had established state residency.

As the start of the school year approached, I was notified that I was on a waiting list of five thousand students for on-campus housing. So I had to fly out to Los Angeles prior to the start of classes to find a place to live. My uncle Bob was kind enough to go with me.

Not long after we arrived in L.A., my mother called and suggested that I go door-to-door asking if anyone in the campus area would allow me to work for them in exchange for room and board. When I told my uncle, he thought I was crazy. He said that the only thing people in that ritzy area were likely to do would be to call the police on me for trespassing!

Nevertheless, I told him I wanted to give it a chance and asked him to turn down the next street. For reasons that are still unknown to him, he did not think we should turn down that street. Instead, he proceeded a block further and made a left turn onto Wyton drive.

About halfway down the block, I saw a woman walking her dog. So I got out of the car, explained my situation, and asked her whether her family could use my help in exchange for room and board. She saw no way that she could help me, but she thought perhaps the people across the street might be interested because she had heard that there

17

had been a death in the family. She pointed to a large, Spanish-looking house across the street.

As I walked toward the house, I noticed that it was guarded by a large swinging gate that I would have to get past just to get to the door of the house. So I thought to myself, if this gate is locked, I am just going to forget about it. As I approached the gate, I noticed that it was unchained and had been left slightly open, so I walked up to the house but was unable to tell where the front door was. Unknowingly, I walked along the side of the house to the rear door. As I passed by the dining room window, I saw a family inside having dinner. There were two elegantly dressed women at the table, two priests, and another gentleman. They were being waited on by a young girl around the age of seven, who was primly dressed and playing hostess. So I thought to myself, I am not going to interrupt this family's dinner with my personal problem. But as I again passed the dining room window on my way out, I became concerned that they might have seen me and mistaken me for a prowler, especially because it was getting dark. So to allay their fear, I thought I had better go back, knock on the door, and politely explain that I had made a mistake. So I walked around back again and knocked on the door.

The woman who answered swung the door wide open and invited me in as though they had been expecting me. And so there I was, standing in front of a captive audience that was anxiously waiting to hear what I had to say. I was so taken back by it that I could do nothing but tell the truth.

Amazingly, this family had been helping UCLA students for years, and they told me that they might have a place for me! As a part of my interview, they asked me to stop at Maria Prima, an assisted living home they had been managing, and introduce myself to the ladies there. When I got back to the car, my uncle said that he had been worried about me and thought for sure they had called the police.

About a week after I returned to Chicago, I received a letter from the family I had met explaining that the student who had been living with them suddenly decided to up and leave. I wound up living with the McCanns until I graduated from college five years later. But that was only the beginning of a long and lasting friendship. Four years later (nine years after the night we first met) the family flew to Chicago for my graduation from medical school and for my wedding.

There are several reasons I am convinced that God arranged my meeting the McCanns. The first is that my uncle, for no logical reason, deliberately passed the street I had asked him to turn on and instead proceeded to Wyton Drive. The second is that there happened to be someone on the street to point to the house where the McCanns were. The third is that the McCanns had for years been offering housing to students and had a well-developed arrangement in place. The fourth is that they actually lived deep in the canyon where I could never have found them had they not been visiting at the home of Mary Creutz that evening. Their visit is also what caused the gate to have been left partially open. The fifth is that this family was perfectly positioned to guide me both academically and spiritually. Dr. McCann was affiliated with the UCLA dental school, which ultimately helped me get into medical school, and his wife, Dr. Kathleen McCann, was a professor of English who would teach me the writing skills that would allow me to share my knowledge and blessings with others through books like this one. But most important, the McCanns were true Christians and the finest people I have ever met.

Motorcycle Prayer for Safety

As I discussed in a previous memoir, I had bought a motorcycle in Chicago just before I flew out to California for the start of classes at UCLA. I had boxed it on a crate and had it shipped to Los Angeles so that it would be waiting for me when I arrived at the home of the McCanns.

Though full of excitement when I arrived and saw it by the mailbox waiting for me, I had real concerns about the safety of riding a motorcycle to school every day. So I made an agreement with God. I said, "Lord, protect me while I am on my motorcycle. If I am ever in danger or in an accident, save me from injury, and I will devote the rest of my life to you."

Before I had had a chance to even sit on the motorcycle, Dr. McCann made wearing a helmet a contingency of living with them. For the first three years, I road safely and even purchased a second motorcycle as a backup given that there was no public transportation out of the canyon. Then came my first brush with death while riding, followed by another.

The first occurred one sunny afternoon as I was riding down Westwood Boulevard in Brentwood. I was going about forty miles per hour when I splashed through a large puddle of oil. From afar, it looked like water, but when I went through it, I knew I was in trouble. With all that oil coating my tires, there was no way I was going to be able to use my breaks without wiping out. The upcoming intersection was Olympic Boulevard—a busy one, and I desperately needed a green light! I remember praying, "Oh God, please let the light be green." It was, but the ordeal was not yet over; I still had enough oil on my tires to make the next intersection no less dangerous. So I again prayed for a green light, and by the grace of God, got another one.

My second brush with death occurred on a bright sunny morning as I was riding to Santa Monica College on the San Diego Freeway. From what seemed like out of nowhere, a car from the far left lane veered sharply in front of me. It happened so quickly that I had not even had time to honk, much less get out of the way. All I could do was brace myself to be hit. Suddenly—boom, and the next thing I knew I was skidding down the freeway on my head with my legs flying up in the air. I can still hear the grinding of the pavement against my helmet as I faced a difficult decision. I realized that I could try to stop myself and risk breaking or losing an arm or leg; or I could remain curled up in a ball and allow myself to roll down the freeway in an effort to protect my body but risk rolling off the edge of the overpass that I knew was under construction and had no guardrail. It's amazing how fast the mind works in a situation like that.

Preferring to live my life whole or not at all, I chose to remain curled up in a ball and allowed myself to tumble down the freeway. So there I went, rolling and skidding on my head over and over again. Although I could have been run over, my greater fear was that of rolling off the edge of the overpass and falling a hundred feet to my death. I can remember just waiting to go into free-fall, as I could sense how close to the edge of the roadway I was moving.

After rolling what seemed like about fifty feet, I came to a stop and managed to stand on my feet. I was so full of adrenaline that I had to visually inspect my body to be sure that all of my parts were there. I remember looking at my legs and counting the number of fingers on each hand. My sweater and pants were partially torn off, but everything else was intact.

When I looked up, the entire freeway was backed up with cars and trucks, and a couple of truck drivers were running toward me. Before they could reach me, a policeman who happened to have been riding behind me on a motorcycle walked up to me and asked if I was all right. I told him I was, and he said, "You're one lucky young man. Wait here, the guy who hit you took off; I'm going after him."

As I stood there, I noticed that I was only ten feet from the edge of the roadway, and my motorcycle was even closer to the edge. I thanked God for saving me and decided right there and then that I would sell both of my motorcycles. My last ride was to the emergency room and then home.

When I arrived back home, I noticed that my brand new Bell helmet—a helmet that my step-father had bought me—had deep gashes in it. I then realized that it had saved my life; or rather that Dr. McCann had saved my life by requiring me to wear it; or rather that God had saved my life by leading me to such a caring family. In any case, the Good Lord had honored my request for protection, and I knew I owed Him the rest of my life in return.

I Kept the Sabbath Day Holy

I learned to read from a children's Bible, and I have been reading the Holy Bible ever since. Consequently, I have always been familiar with the teachings of Scripture. But it was not until my first year of college that I began to feel a conviction to keep the Sabbath day holy. That is, to keep Sundays free of all activities except for rest, worship, and prayer. College was actually the most difficult time for me to start because I had classes during the week, and I was working for my room and board on Saturdays. Consequently, Sundays were my only day to catch up on my studies. What is more, I was a premedical student at one of the most competitive schools in the country, and I often had exams on Monday mornings. So there I was, no longer able to use Sundays "productively." Instead, I would come home from church in the morning and spend the rest of the day fretting about all the time I was wasting by resting on Sunday. I kept questioning the wisdom of what I was doing.

Yet I knew my faith in God was being tested. As the weeks went by, I gradually began to find things to do on Sundays that were more productive than fretting. I began to socialize a little after church and watch some golf on television in the afternoon. Then I would do some Bible reading in the evening and retire to bed early with the intent of getting a fresh start on Monday morning.

Surprisingly, my academic performance was not adversely affected. As I took notice of that, I gradually began to look forward to Sundays as a day when I could leave all my worries behind with the assurance that everything would be okay. Eventually, that became a strict rule: I did not permit myself to worry or even problem-solve on Sundays, regardless of what I faced on Monday morning. Thus, Sunday became a sacred day on which I was protected from all my problems, and that made it truly restful.

Eventually, small miracles began to occur. For instance, I began to earn my highest exam scores on Monday mornings. In fact, on more than one occasion, I had a score of one hundred percent and the highest grade in the class on a Monday morning exam. Even more amazingly, I was able to keep the Sabbath day holy throughout medical school and hold my own academically there too.

During those years, I would take Holy Communion to the elderly at a nearby assisted living facility on Sunday afternoons following church services. In the process, I met some wonderful people, including Gertrude Sullivan, the woman who founded Boy's Town with Fr. Flanagan. She was over one hundred years old at the time that I met her, and she inspired me with her youthful spirit and words of wisdom, as did several other residents there.

Even after I graduated from medical school and started private practice, the Lord found a way to allow me to continue to keep the Sabbath rest. All the younger doctors in the Department of Psychiatry at Waukesha Memorial Hospital, which was where I started out in private practice, was expected to be available by page at all times. But shortly after I had joined the staff, my senior partner asked me if I would cover for him on Saturdays. In an effort to be gracious, I told him I would. He then told me he would cover for me on Sundays! That was quite extraordinary given that he was a senior partner in our group and a Christian himself. But the real power of the Sabbath was just beginning to be revealed, as we will see later.

Statistics Class Miracle

As a pre-medical student at UCLA, I could not afford anything less than an "A" grade in any of my classes. But just as I was getting ready to apply to medical school, I found myself in trouble going into the final exam in statistics. I really did not like statistics, and the class was giving me fits from the start. On the first three exams, I had two scores that were on the borderline between an "A" and a "B", and one score that was so low that I knew it would keep me from getting an "A" in the class even if I were to get a perfect score on the final exam.

I was seriously thinking, oh Lord, what am I going to do? Then the professor announced that he was considering dropping everyone's lowest exam score and increasing the weight of the final exam proportionately. I couldn't believe my ears. No UCLA professor had ever offered to do such a thing. To drop an exam score was simply unheard of. A few days later, the professor allowed the class to vote on it. Of course, even as he was calling for the vote, I was praying that the class would vote in favor of the idea.

My prayer was answered; the class wound up voting in favor of dropping the lowest exam score. But even with that, I knew I would need to ace the final exam in order to have any chance of getting an "A" in the class.

Unfortunately, I did not do very well on the final. As I turned in my exam, I could sense that I had probably gotten a "B" at best. So I went home really upset that weekend. In my angst, I spent all day Saturday obsessing about the accuracy of every answer I gave.

Finally, I started thinking to myself, I need some real help. So I began to pray for an "A". In my logical mind, I knew that no prayer in the world was going to change my exam score; the score was what it was. But as I reminded myself that with God all things are possible, I continued to pray. I spent all day Saturday that weekend trying to replace my worries with faith, yet I remained very anxious and upset. Late in the day, I finally had a breakthrough—my angst started to be replaced by peace, joy, and gratitude to God for hearing my prayer. When I awoke on Sunday morning, I still had the peace that I felt on Saturday night. For the remainder of Sunday, I battled my logical mind and put forth a sustained effort to maintain my faith. Amazingly, I was successful and enjoyed a restful, peaceful night that carried through to Monday morning.

Just before class on Monday morning, all the students in statistics were anxiously awaiting the professor's arrival with our exams. Then one of the students shouted, "He's here!" And everyone flocked to the window to watch the professor walk from his car into the building. I just remained seated, trying not to let anything shake my faith. Five minutes later, the professor walked into the classroom with the exams.

Students quickly lined up at his desk to get their test scores, but I remained seated, trying to maintain my composure. When all the students had gotten their exams, the professor walked up to my desk and handed me my exam.

When I looked at the score, I saw a "B-". Had I not been trying to maintain my faith, I surely would have gone into a panic. But thanks to the faith that I had been working so hard to maintain, I remained calm. Trusting more in God than in what my eyes were telling me, I thought to myself, surely there must be some mistake; the professor must have graded my exam wrong. Now what caused me to think there had been a grading error, I do not know because I had never jumped to such a conclusion before. In any case, I calmly started paging through my exam, searching for any mistakes. About midway through it, I noticed that the professor had failed to count one of the scores on a subsection. Despite this amazing discovery, I kept my composure and continued to work through the rest of the exam in search of any other grading errors. The remainder of the exam had been properly graded. I then calmly walked up to the professor's desk and told him that there was a mistake on my score. "What do you mean?" he retorted; "I've been teaching here for twenty years and have never made a grading error." But when he looked at the page, it was quite obvious that he had not added one of the sub-scores. "Well I'll be darned," he said, "I did make a mistake." So he corrected my score and handed my exam back to me. Trying to maintain my faith, I continued to stand there. Then he asked, "Why are you standing there?" Before I could say anything, he said, "Oh, you want to see if it changed your grade. I don't think so," he said, "But I'll check." So he looked to see where my exam score fell on the curve in his grading book. Then he said, "No, I didn't think so," and handed my exam back to me. I was so focused on trying to maintain my faith that I did not respond. Then he said, "Wait, let me double check." As he looked again at the curve in his book, he said, "Wait a minute, that does just put you into the "A" category... by one point." He then changed my grade and handed my exam back to me. I politely thanked him and sat down.

That was the only time in twenty-five years of schooling that I had ever thought to go through an exam looking for a grading error. There is no doubt in my mind that God had given me the idea to do it. My faith had allowed me to receive God's guidance and look through my exam for a mistake that the Lord alone knew was there. Of course, had there not been a grading error, I am sure God would have found another way to reward my faith.

Healed by the Blood of Christ

As a UCLA student, I would sometimes serve as a Eucharistic Minister at the campus Newman Center. By that I mean that I would sometimes help distribute Holy Communion during church services.

During my second year of college, I developed a protracted stomachache for unknown reasons. Being in good general health, I kept thinking it would go away, but it persisted for weeks. Eventually, I came to the point of feeling that I needed to see a doctor.

That Sunday at mass, I was distributing Holy Communion, and because my stomach was aching, I dreaded the thought of having to consume the remainder of the wine in my chalice. I had never had a drink in my life, and that was no time for me to start experimenting.

As it turned out, my Chalice was still full at the end of mass. Not knowing what effect all that wine would have on my upset stomach, I found myself having to choose between my logic and my faith. My logic told me not to drink it; but my faith reminded me that it was the blood of my Lord and Savior Jesus Christ, by which I am healed.

Choosing to honor my faith, I reverently consumed all the wine in the chalice. Though my logic kept telling me that it was going to make me worse, my stomachache immediately disappeared and never returned.

We Reap What We Sow

One of my colleagues once told me that he never went out of his way for strangers, and by the same token, strangers never went out of their way for him. The interesting thing about it, he said, was that those who did not help him were not the same persons who he did not help.

My personal experience has been the flip side of his observation. I have often gone out of my way for strangers, and strangers have often gone out of their way for me. The interesting thing is that those who have helped me were not necessarily the same ones who I helped. It is a testimony to the Lord's teaching: you will reap what you sow. And our deeds often return to us in the most unexpected ways.

Late one night, I got stranded with a flat tire as I was driving through an inner city ghetto. I thought for sure that whoever saw me was going to take my car rather than help me fix it. But amazingly, not one but two separate individuals pulled over to help me without my even having to ask for help. Instead of doing me harm, they teamed up to push my car to a nearby gas station. And as if that weren't providential enough, the guys at the gas station fixed my tire for free!

On another occasion, I was sitting at the Registrar's Office at UCLA eating a sandwich, when a street person walked up to me and asked for some change. I told him I didn't have any but offered him one of my sandwiches. He took the sandwich and said, "God bless you."

As I watched him slowly make his way to the end of the long corridor, I was thinking about what a sacrifice I had made because I was really hungry and still had a long day ahead of me. I was just hoping that he was going to eat that sandwich rather than throw it away.

As I continued to eat my other sandwich, I noticed that he had turned around and was slowly walking back toward me. After a few minutes, he had returned to where I was sitting. He then reached out and handed my sandwich back to me saying, "You take this, you need it; but God bless you."

You Can't Cheat God

Miracles don't always come in the form of pleasant surprises or answered prayer requests. Sometimes they come in the form of powerful lessons.

One day I needed to run into a convenience store on a crowded street in Los Angeles. There was nowhere to legally park my motorcycle, but I did see a small no-parking zone right in front of the store.

As I was parking my motorcycle there, I felt God say to me, "You know you shouldn't park there." But I thought to myself, I'm gonna get away with it because there's no way a policeman will have time to see my motorcycle and write me a ticket in the two short minutes that I'll be in this store. Not only that, but the parking space was located in front of a window in the part of the store where the item I needed was shelved. It would allow me to check on my motorcycle at the same time that I was grabbing the item I needed! So I again thought to myself, I know that this is wrong, but I'll definitely get away with it.

So I darted into the store and even checked on my motorcycle as I grabbed the item I needed. As expected, there were no police around. Less than two minutes later, I came rushing out of the store, only to find a police officer standing next to my motorcycle writing a ticket. I couldn't believe it! So I said, "Officer, I just ran into the store for a minute, and I'm leaving right now." She said, "I'm sorry, but I've already started writing your ticket."

The moral of the story: you can't cheat God; you can only cheat yourself.

The Danger of Pride

Pride did me in again during my senior year in college as I sat on the UCLA campus lawn with something very important I had just received in the mail—the results of my MCAT (Medical College Aptitude Test). I will never forget the fear and trembling with which I checked those all-important exam scores. As I sat there on the lawn amidst hundreds of other students in the midday sun, I slowly began to slide the insert of box scores out of the envelope. The exam consisted of five subsections: basic science, chemistry, biology, physics, and reading comprehension. I knew that I would need a good score on each section if I were to have any chance of being accepted to medical school. So I said a prayer and looked at the first score: eightieth percentile in basic science—good enough. The the second score: eighty-fourth percentile in chemistry—another good score. Then biology: eighty-sixth percentile—even better. In physics, I couldn't believe my eyes—ninety ninth percentile! That meant I had scored better than ninety-nine percent of all the students in the country who had taken the exam. At that point, I felt so proud of myself that I did not think any more prayers were necessary and that I no longer needed God's help. Then I presumptuously checked my last score—reading comprehension. To my chagrin, it was extremely low. The only thought in my mind as my heart sank into the pit of my stomach was, you don't need God anymore, ha. I had the sense that that was going to haunt me for a long time and possibly even keep me out of medical school. All I could do at that point was beg God for forgiveness. A year later, I saw the evidence of His forgiveness!

+ + +

✝

CHAPTER 4

—⁓⁂⁓—

MIRACLES DURING
MEDICAL SCHOOL AND RESIDENCY

A Risky Transfer

While home for the summer after my first year of medical school at Creighton University, I went out dancing with a girl I had met in high school. I had not seen her since graduation, but she wrote to me periodically while I was away at college. We wound up seeing each other every week that summer in Chicago, and we wrote to each other frequently after I returned to school at Creighton in the Fall.

After about four or five months, she explained in a letter that the long-distance relationship was too hard for her to bear and that she really needed me to be closer. I had been about midway through my second year of medical school at the time, and I thought to myself, if I were to transfer to a school in the Chicago area, this would be the time to do it. But it was a risky proposition. I had worked so hard to get into medical school, and things were going very well for me at Creighton. I had been doing well academically, I had gotten to know many my professors, and I was well-liked by the Dean. I was also popular among my classmates, having recently been nominated for class president. On the other hand, transferring to a school in the Chicago area would bring me back to my home town, where I wanted to start a practice after I finished medical school.

As I started to look at schools in the Chicago area, I turned my attention to one school in particular—the University of Chicago. Not only was it in the part of the city where Maggie was studying dentistry but it was also where I had been accepted to college and would have gone had there not been so many advantages to playing college baseball at UCLA.

But when I called the Dean's office to inquire about transferring, the secretary told me that the deadline for accepting transfer applications had already passed. Not willing to give up that easily, I called back again and asked to speak with Dean Ceithaml. Surprisingly, the secretary put me through to him. "Dean Ceithaml," I said, "my name is Michael Binder. I am a second-year medical student at Creighton University, and I would like to transfer to the University Chicago at the end of this year." He said, "Didn't my secretary tell you that the deadline for transfer applications has passed?" I said, "He did, but I really want to come to the University of Chicago." He said, "You really want to come to this school?" My answer was a decisive YES. So he asked me what kind of grades I was getting at Creighton. I told him I was averaging a "B+". He said, "That's pretty good for medical school. And you really want to come here, ha?" Again I said, YES. So he said, "I will have my secretary send you an application, but return it directly to me. I said, "Thank you so much, Dr. "Ceithaml."

Though I was overjoyed by the opportunity to complete the application for transfer, I was still apprehensive about taking such a risk. The thought of leaving a school where I was enjoying so much success was difficult for me. I was also concerned about the effect my request would have on my relationship with the Dean at Creighton. But Dean Ceithaml had given me this golden opportunity, and I felt committed to going through with it.

Now the last hurdle I faced was that of telling the Dean at Creighton what I wanted to do and why. I began to think of all kinds of reasons to give him, all of them academic, of course. But none of them were true. On the other hand, the truth did not seem to be a very acceptable reason to transfer.

After mulling it over for awhile, I still wasn't sure what I was going to tell the Dean Pancoe. Even as I waited outside the office to meet with him, I still had not decided. Then, at the last moment, I said, "Oh God, please help me." And the Lord answered softly, "If you want My help, tell him the truth; or, you can go it alone, and tell him whatever you want."

As I turned the corner to go into the Dean's office, I thought to myself: better to put my trust in God than in my logic; I'll just tell him the truth. A moment later, there I was, standing in front of Dean Pancoe's desk about to make a complete fool of myself by telling him the sorry truth about why I wanted to transfer to another medical school.

30

"Michael," he said, "How can I help you?" "Hi Dean Pancoe, I would like to transfer medical schools," I said. "Oh...where would you like to go?" he asked, looking a little perplexed. I said, "The University of Chicago." "Good school," he said, "but why do you want to transfer?" At that point, I felt myself about to go from six feet tall to the size of an ant. Trying to force out the words, I said, "Because of a relationship. I am seeing a woman in Chicago who I would like to marry." So he said, "Well, I'll have you know that we rarely allow transfers; but when we do, it is only in the case of a long-distance relationship. Had you given me any other reason, I would not even have been able to consider your request. But if a transfer is what you really want, I will do what I can to help you."

About three weeks later, Dean Pancoe called me into his office. He said he had received a call from Dean Ceithaml at the University of Chicago. He told me they called him the "Dean of Deans" because he was the most respected Dean in the nation. Dean Pancoe continued, "He said he wanted to know what kind of student you were. I told him that if they did not want to accept you, it would be fine with us. And Dean Ceithaml said, 'We'll take him.' And that," he said, "was the extent of the conversation." I thanked Dean Pancoe, and he said, "We'll miss you, but I hope you'll be happy there."

That, however, was not the end of the story. Just before Dean Ceithaml rendered his final decision, he called me at home to inquire about the low reading score on my MCAT. I told him I could not understand why I had scored so low because I had tested reasonably well in reading comprehension on my practice exams and my reading ability seemed on par with other students in my medical school class. Having misunderstood what I said, Dean Ceithaml replied, "Oh...you mean you're reading ability is even better than other students in your class?" At that point, I so much wanted to just say "yes" and be done with it. But instead, I corrected his misunderstanding and said, "No, I mean that my reading ability is just average." Sounding let down, he said, "Oh, I see. Thank you very much," and he hung up.

The call left me feeling so upset that I threw myself on my bed and began to cry. I kept thinking to myself that all I had to have done was to have said "yes" to that last question, and I would have been in. But I had to blow the whole thing by being honest.

A few minutes later, my grandmother came into my room and asked me why I was so upset. She consoled me by telling me that she had once

31

been in a similar situation. She too had told the truth when it was difficult, and she wound up getting the job.

Nevertheless, I continued to feel pretty down as I prepared to return to Creighton to study for my second-year Board exam. I had lingering fears that my reading score was going to prevent me from being accepted for transfer. Worse yet, it was threatening to interfere with my preparation for the Board exam. I thought to myself, I really have to be focused in preparing for this exam, and the last thing I need is a call from home saying that my request for transfer has been denied.

So I thought about not letting anyone in my family know where in Omaha I would be spending the next few weeks preparing for my exam. But then I thought, what if there were an emergency at home and my family needed to contact me? So I reluctantly decided to give my grandmother a telephone number where I could be reached.

After a week and a half of intensive study at a house I had rented near school with three of my classmates, I was starting to feel burned out. Just as I was beginning to lose concentration, I received a call from my grandmother saying that the Dean from the University Chicago had called and asked for me. She said that he wanted to tell me personally that I had been accepted! She went on to say that my acceptance letter was in the mail. The call had filled my sails and renewed my energy. I can distinctly remember going outside, looking up at the clouds, and thanking God over and over again.

Later, I thought about what a good thing it was that I had given my grandmother my telephone number. Her good news phone call was my reward for thinking of others and for being honest even when it was difficult. My excitement about being accepted to the prestigious Pritzker School of Medicine had given me the emotional boost I needed to finish preparing for and take the longest and most intensive exam I had been faced with up to that point in my education. What is more, it was an examination I needed to pass as a contingency of my acceptance to the University of Chicago.

I ended up passing the exam, but I'm not sure I could have done it without the help of God, Dean Ceithaml, Dean Pancoe, and my grandmother's good news phone call.

The Danger of Passing Judgment

Although my faith in God has opened the door for many miracles, I have not always been obedient, and my disobedience has robbed me of some of God's blessings and protection.

While I was a medical student at the University of Chicago, one of my classmates told me that he had a scheduling conflict and asked me if I would switch rotations with him. It was a simple request and one that I would have had no problem granting if it weren't for the fact that I didn't trust him. I had the impression that he was a selfish guy who took advantage of people. So I passed judgment and refused him just because I thought he might be up to something.

As it turned out, the teaching professor on my rotation was a very different thinker than I was and made me repeat the rotation. She also assigned me to the Student Health Department as part of my remedial work. On the last day of the rotation in Student Health, I examined a patient who was suspected of having the chickenpox. Although I knew I was at risk for becoming infected, I thought I was safe based upon the assumption that I had had the chickenpox as a child.

Well, my assumption was wrong. Eleven days after I examined the patient, I saw the first pock marks on my arm, and within less than a week, I was covered with chickenpox. I counted over one hundred pockmarks on my forehead alone! Fortunately, I had just started a one-month research rotation under the tutelage of Dr. Michael McCann in Los Angeles. Consequently, I was not only in good hands when I got sick, but I was able to complete my assignment despite being in quarantine because I was working on a research project.

Even after the pox cleared, I remained pretty sick for several weeks. After I recovered, I was reassigned to the rotation I had failed, and as fate would have it, the attending was the professor I would have had had I agreed to switch rotations with my classmate. As it turned out, that professor and I communicated well, and I passed with flying colors.

The beauty of the story is that God disciplined me while demonstrating His providence and protection. He placed me in the hands of my longtime mentor and friend Dr. Michael McCann when I got sick, while at the same time allowing me to suffer the consequences of passing judgment on my classmate. As it is written, "Judge not, that ye be not judged," and the son who the father loves he does not spare the rod. Matthew 7:1, KJV.

Blessed are the Peacemakers

When I was Resident in psychiatry, the two Residents on duty would split the overnight shift. One would work from 2:00 a.m. to 5:00 a.m., and the other would work from 5:00 a.m. to 8:00 a.m. Nearly everyone preferred the second shift because it was usually the quieter of the two, so we would take turns choosing shifts.

Well this particular night, it was my turn to choose, so I chose the second shift. But the Resident I was on with claimed that I had gotten to choose the last time we had worked together. So I said to him, "No, I remember distinctly that you chose the last time." Well he disagreed, and we started to argue. Seeing that we weren't getting anywhere and that the argument was beginning to turn ugly, I said, "That's okay, you can have the preferred shift."

Of course, I was pretty upset about having to make the concession, but I did it in an effort to keep the peace. With that, I can remember saying a little prayer that God would reward me for my sacrifice.

That night at 11:00 p.m., I went up to the call room fully expecting to be awoken in the middle of the night to see the usual crowd of boisterous patients that started coming from the bars at around 2:00 a.m. But instead, I awoke to the bright morning sun at 7:00 a.m. I had slept soundly through the entire night, not even receiving a telephone call!

When I went down to the emergency department to sign out, I saw the other Resident slaving away, trying to keep up with the long line of patients that apparently arrived in a wave just after my shift had ended. The staff later agreed that it was probably the largest influx of patients we had ever had in the psychiatric crisis service! And so it is written, "Say not thou, I will recompense evil; but wait on the Lord, and he shall save thee." Proverbs 20:22, KJV.

He Saved Me From Myself

Of the twenty-five years I have spent in the educational system, no examination was as intimidating and stressful as my oral Board examination in psychiatry. The exam is a one-day event in which two examiners who you have never met select a patient from the psychiatric ward and watch you conduct a psychiatric evaluation. What makes the exam so stressful is that you have no idea what kind of patient you are going to get. You are also unaccustomed to having two critics sitting in on a meeting that is normally private, just between you and the patient. Under the weight of this stress, the student must remember all the information the patient provides during the interview and present it to the examiners in an organized formate, followed by a discussion of the diagnosis, treatment, and prognosis for the patient, including a discussion of the various treatment options available. The examiners can then ask questions about the case and biopsychosocial issues relevant to it.

Each year, only about half the students pass. Added to this was the stress of knowing that I would not get a second chance, a second chance, that is, at lifetime board certification. The year I took the exam was the last that the American Board of Psychiatry and Neurology would allow those who passed to be exempt from any further testing for the rest of their lives. So the students who took the exam that year were under far more pressure than at any other time that the examinations had been administered either before or since.

In an effort to desensitize myself to the stress and hone my skills, I had set up a series of mock Board exams with some of my professors and their patients. But even on the practice exams, I was much more nervous than I had hoped I would be. In fact, the stress of preparing for and taking the practice exams was so great that I had to push myself just to do them.

My stress over the whole thing was magnified when I received notice that my Board exam had been scheduled for a Sunday, which is a holy day of obligation for me. I had not worked or studied on the Sabbath day for the preceding nine years, and with such an important exemption on the line, I wasn't sure what to do.

What I did know was that I was going to need God's help with the exam, and so I made obedience to His word my priority. So I wrote a letter to the National Board of Medical Examiners explaining my religious beliefs and asked that my examination be moved to a different day of the week. Of course, I was taking the risk that the rescheduling process could push me into the following year's exam cycle, which would have robbed me of the chance at lifetime Board exemption status. Also, with the field of psychiatry being largely secular, I had fears that my religious beliefs could be held against me. But trusting more in God's providence than my logic, I went ahead and mailed the letter. About a month later, I received a reply saying that my examination had been rescheduled for Saturday morning of the same weekend.

Knowing that good concentration was critical to my success on the exam, I knew that I had to get a good night's sleep. The problem is that sleep can't be forced, so the very thought that I had to have it only added to my stress, which, in turn, made sleep that much more difficult. Though I thought about taking a sleeping pill, I did not think it would be morally right. If nothing else, my moral conviction spared me the worry that a sedative could have lingering effects that could affect my performance on the exam. Then again, I knew that even if I did sleep well, there was no way I was going to be able to concentrate well enough to pass the exam; I just felt too much pressure.

Seeing that I was my own worst enemy, I knew that I had to turn it all over to God. So I said, "Lord, you know that if you leave this up to me, I am going to blow it...I assure you, I am going to blow it! The only way I will be able to stay calm enough to pass this exam is if you take charge of me. So I am going to put it all in your hands. It's gonna be none of me, and all of you!" So with that clear understanding, I boldly but humbly went forth to take the exam.

As the examiners, the patient, and I were getting seated in the room, I could see that the patient was angry and agitated. Her first words to me after all of us got seated were: "I'm not talking to you!" And she just sat there with her arms folded in defiance. Miraculously, I kept my wits about me, and the four of us just sat there quietly as I did my best to be considerate of her feelings. After about five minutes, the patient broke her silence and angrily said, "Well what do you want to ask me?" And so the conversation began.

As it turned out, the examiners were really impressed with the way I handled the awkward situation and the amount of information I managed to obtain from the patient. As we were leaving the room, one of the examiners winked at me and whispered, nice job.

In retrospect, I realized that God had not only carried me through the exam, He also gave me a patient that drew out my best qualities— patience, kindness, and compassion—all qualities that were given to me from above. I also realized that what made that patient assignment possible was my request to change the date of my examination, a request that I had made in obedience to God. Thus, God reached out to me with His helping hand, but my obedience to His word is what enabled me to take hold of it.

+ + +

✝

CHAPTER 5

—◦◦✠◦◦—

MIRACLES IN MY FAMILY LIFE

The Golden Gum-ball

When my daughter was very little, she was extremely sensitive. Although my wife and I gave her a lot of attention and treated her very delicately, she remained anxious and insecure. I can remember nights when I would read her a bedtime story, only to have her begin to cry and tell me that she felt that nobody loved her.

Not knowing what else to do, I asked the Lord to help her. He responded by directing us to a wonderful Waldorf school called Prairie Hill. There, Tammy had the good fortune of being assigned the most gentle loving teacher my wife and I could ever hope for. But as much as that helped, Tammy continued to feel somewhat insecure.

Then one day, she put a quarter into a gum ball machine at a restaurant where my wife sometimes took the kids, and out came the golden gum-ball! There was a sign on top of the machine that said the recipient of the golden gum-ball would win an all-expenses paid family vacation to Disney World, Florida. My wife and I were skeptical and thought there must have been some strings attached. But when my wife called the telephone number on the insert of the golden gum-ball wrapper, she was told that the airline tickets as well as five days at any one of Disney's five-star resorts were included. We were also instructed to go to our local Disney store to claim two hundred dollars in Disney spending money!

By that time, the kids had seen "Willy Wonka and the Chocolate Factory" several times, and even my daughter agreed that the prize she won was far greater than just one day in a chocolate factory.

After a few days in the magical place that Disney World is for a five-year-old, Tammy seemed to have forgotten her fears and insecurities.

To be sure, she got the royal treatment from Mickey, Minnie, Goofy, and all the other loving characters who were bigger than life to her. All the while, I reminded her that the trip was God's special gift to her.

She returned from the trip a changed person. In his own magical way, God had answered my prayer and Tammy's need by giving her a very special form of love and attention, a form that was just right for her and which we were able to enjoy as a family. Today, she is the most confident, independent person I know.

God Knows Best

When my wife became pregnant with our first child, I prayed for a son. I imagined myself watching him in Little League and us playing baseball and golf together. But my wife did not give birth to a boy; we had a baby girl. As it turned out, I so enjoyed Tammy's sweetness and the magical moments we shared reading bedtime stories and catching butterflies that when my wife got pregnant a second time, I prayed for another girl. But near the end of the pregnancy, I had a dream about my grandmother's late uncle, the renowned Bible scholar, Dr. George M. Lamsa. In the dream, I saw uncle Lamsa laying in his death bed with my son's priest praying over him. Suddenly, uncle Lamsa sat up in bed, turned his head, and looked strait at me. That was where the dream ended.

After I told my mother and my grandmother about the dream, my mother shared it with a church friend who was known for her ability to interpret dreams. She said that my wife was pregnant and would have a son who would follow in the footsteps of Dr. Lamsa and continue his work. Accordingly, she said that we were to name him after Dr. Lamsa.

At the time, we were still unsure whether the baby was a boy or a girl, but the ultrasonographer had told my wife that it looked like a girl. Well, her impression was wrong; my wife gave birth to a son as foretold by the dream interpreter.

My wife and I agreed to name him John Michael Lamsa—John, after his grandfather; Michael, after his father; and Lamsa, after his great great uncle. But unlike my daughter, who was very gentle and cooperative as she was growing up, my son was feisty and oppositional. I would have to say that the only promise of holiness I saw in him was when he took a stand with an unbelieving classmate and insisted that God was real.

But true to his nature, Johnny threatened to beat up the boy if he ever again heard him say that there was no God. So at the outset, it didn't look too much like Johnny was going to fulfill the prophecy that he would follow in the footsteps of uncle Lamsa. However, I prayed that God would give him the grace to change his attitude.

Then, as my son approached his teens, he started to have severe and embarrassing panic attacks that gradually led to changes in his attitude that have been nothing short of miraculous. He became patient, obedient, and respectful. He also became increasingly spiritual and an ardent but peaceable defender of the faith. Today, he is the most wonderful son a father could ever hope for and my best friend. And while God indeed has answered my prayer for a son with whom I could enjoy playing baseball and golf, He has blessed me with something far greater—a son with whom I can praise God and share the Gospel—a son who I truly believe is destined to continue Dr. Lamsa's work.

The Wisdom of Love

When we were living in Wisconsin, my family and I took a vacation to Oshkosh. Looking forward to the long weekend, my wife and I had planned things for her to do, things for me to do, and things for the kids to do. My wife enjoyed tanning, I enjoyed golfing, and the kids enjoyed everything else.

But as I was dropping my wife and kids off at a shopping mall on the afternoon that we had planned for me to play golf, my daughter suddenly began to cry and say, "No papa, don't go; stay with us." My wife tried to settle her down and explain that it was what we had planned. But in desperation, my daughter kept begging me to stay with her.

At that point I realized that I had to choose between my daughter and myself. Though my wife and I had agreed that I would play golf that afternoon, I could see that if I left, my daughter would take it as a rejection. So out of love for her, I bit the bullet and told her I would stay. She immediately threw her arms around me and said, "Thank you, Papa; thank you! thank you! thank you!"

Moments later, raindrops began to form on the car windshield. By the time we came out of the shopping mall two hours later, it was pouring outside, and I realized that I would not have been able to play golf anyway. Boy was I glad that I had chosen to love!

That evening, my family decided that since I had made the sacrifice, they would allow me to play golf the following afternoon. Wouldn't you know it, the weather turned out to be spectacular—sunny skies, temperatures in the mid seventies, and virtually no wind—a perfect day for golf!

Lost Cat Found

For many years, we had three cats. One winter night I pulled into the garage, and at the same time, my wife opened the house-door to the garage to greet me.

The next morning, one of our cats was missing. After some thought, we came to the conclusion that she had gotten out when I pulled into the garage the night before. We were really worried because the temperature had dipped below zero overnight, and odds were that she would freeze to death if we did not find her soon.

After looking around for awhile, I started to get the feeling that finding the cat was going to be next to impossible. There were just too many places she could have gone. Worse yet, there were large drainage pipes that traveled beneath the streets, any one of which would have been an attractive place for her to hide for shelter.

Knowing how much the cat meant to my wife, I said a prayer that God would help us find her. About five minutes later, my wife rushed out of the house with some flyers she had made. As she was starting to post them on the porches of the homes along the street, I suddenly heard her cry out, "I found her! I found her!"

When I heard it, I could not believe my ears. I immediately praised God for answering my prayer. The cat had been hiding underneath a bench on the porch of one of our neighbors. It's hard to believe that my wife was even able to see her there. And not only that, the cat was in perfectly fine.

Faith and a Free Cruz

About fifteen years ago, my wife and I received an invitation for a seven-day, all expenses paid Bahamas cruise. Our only obligation was to attend a three-hour seminar on the last day of the trip. My wife thought the offer was a scam, but I saw it as a gift from God and a golden opportunity for a much-needed vacation. So I told her we should go.

As it turned out, we spent the first three days in a beautiful hotel in Fort Lauderdale, Florida. The weather was great, the food was free, and the kids had fun playing in the pool all day. On the fourth day, our itinerary had us drive to Miami Beach, where we boarded a cruz ship and spent the next three days laying in the sun and dining in the middle of the Caribbean. All meals were included, no gratuities were accepted, and we enjoyed some of the finest food we had ever had. It's a very unique and special feeling to sit down to a formal dinner while afloat in the middle of the ocean. Although there were plenty of opportunities to gamble, I refrained, keeping to a commitment to God that I will discuss later.

We spent the last two days of the trip in another beautiful setting and did not pay a penny for anything! After all was said and done, we estimated the cost of the trip to be around five thousand dollars—no scam but a gift from God. That's how far a little faith will get you.

Miracle of the Monarchs

When my daughter was little, she loved butterflies. She particularly loved Monarchs, and there were many times when I ran around catching them with her. For a time, I even carried a net in my golf bag so that if I saw a Monarch or Swallowtail on the golf course, I could catch it and bring it home to her.

Then one day I thought to myself, imagine if my daughter could watch a caterpillar metamorphosize into a big, beautiful Monarch butterfly. The question was, where would we find a caterpillar that would turn into a Monarch butterfly? And what would it look like?

So we did some research and learned what species of caterpillar we would have to find and what it looked like. The Monarch Butterfly Caterpillar is a chubby green insect about the size of your little finger with black, white, and yellow stripes arranged in a repeating pattern of rings around its body. We also learned that Monarch Butterfly Caterpillars feed on the milkweed plant. So we had to figure out what milkweed was and where to find it.

Well one summer day while my wife was participating in a horse show, my daughter and I went to a field around back where there happened to have been an enormous patch of milkweed. I felt certain that we would find more than one Monarch Butterfly Caterpillar in all that milkweed. But despite hours of searching, we found nothing.

During the following weeks, we continued to look for milkweed and the caterpillars but had no luck finding either one.

Then one day after a round of golf, I spotted a large patch of milkweed just beyond the golf course parking lot. I knew there must have been some Monarch Butterfly Caterpillars around because I had seen several Monarchs fly across the golf course while I had been golfing. So I went over and started looking through the milkweed, absolutely determined to find a caterpillar for my daughter. But once again, I wasn't finding anything.

Determined to return home with a caterpillar, I asked God to help me. "Oh Lord," I said, "I have looked everywhere. Please help me find one of those caterpillars." It was no different than the time I had asked Him to help me find a shark's tooth. So with full confidence, I resumed my slow, methodical search in that same patch of milkweed. But after nearly an hour, I still had not found anything. So I thought to myself, this is the first time in my life that I have prayed with faith and seen my prayer go unanswered. Sadly, I walked back across the parking lot, got into my car, and drove home. As I was driving, I kept wondering why the Lord had not answered my prayer. Was He trying to protect my daughter from something? Were those caterpillars poisonous? Had she just come home with a new pet? I just couldn't figure it out.

About a week later, I was seeing patient in my office, and as the session was ending, he casually started talking about how his children loved catching bugs. I said, "Yea, my kids do to, but my daughter loves butterflies; she likes the Monarchs." He said, "My kids love those too." Then I said, "My daughter and I have been looking for a Monarch Butterfly Caterpillar." And he said, "Oh yea, my kids those too; in fact, they are out catching them right now."

Then I thought to myself, I don't think he really understands what I'm talking about. So I said, "No, I'm talking about Monarch Butterfly Caterpillars. They are a specific type of caterpillar that turns into a Monarch butterfly. And he said, "Oh yes, I know; that's what my kids catch all the time." I said, "You must be kidding." He said, "No...would you like me to have them give your daughter some?" I said, "No, don't ask them to give any of theirs away. But maybe you could ask them to catch one for her." He said, "I will." Then he left.

I just dismissed the conversation as idle talk until about an hour later when my secretary called into my office and said, "Ah...Dr. Binder. Can you come out to the waiting room? There's a gentleman with two children here to see you. They have two big boxes of bugs." I thought to myself, I can't believe it. When I went out to the waiting room, my patient was waiting for me with his two children. Each of the kids had an egg crate box full of milkweed with several giant Monarch Butterfly Caterpillars feeding on it.

So the little girl started telling me how to care for the caterpillars and what to expect. She said that most would probably die but that in eleven days a few would turn into butterflies. She went on to give me specific instructions for caring for them. As she was talking, I noticed that her brother was holding a jar of caterpillars that were about half the size of the ones in the boxes. When I asked the kids why their caterpillars were smaller than the ones they caught for my daughter, they just shrugged their shoulders and said, "We don't know, that's what we found."

So I thanked them and told them how I had asked God to find a Monarch Butterfly Caterpillar for my daughter. Seeing what they had in the boxes, I told them that they were the angels God had sent in response to my prayer. Their eyes became the size of an owl's as I discussed the miracle and their part in it.

After work, I took the caterpillars home and followed the instructions the kids had given me. Within a few days, all the caterpillars had turned into black buds that were hanging upside down. If it hadn't been for a thin band of bright golden beads that had formed around the collar of each chrysalis, I would have mistaken all of them for dead. Approximately eleven days later, the chrysalises began to open into big, beautiful, Monarch butterflies, just as the kids had foretold. Of the thirteen caterpillars, nine had survived! After all the butterflies had fully expanded their wings, my daughter took them outside and let them go.

Three weeks later, my patient and his kids invited my kids to go caterpillar hunting in the same patch of milkweed where they had found all the caterpillars. On the day we got together, were a posse of six persons hunting for caterpillars. But after two hours of an intensive search, all we had found was one small, half-dead caterpillar. Though everyone was disappointed, it highlighted the wonder of the miracle that had taken place three weeks earlier.

Our failure to find caterpillars also turned into an opportunity for my son to have his own dream come true. Johnny loved to fish, and it turned out that right across the way from the milkweed patch was a fish pond loaded with home-grown Bass. So, having given up on finding the caterpillars, we went fishing. All the kids caught Bass of all sizes, and my son was in heaven!!!

In the end, my simple prayer had blossomed into two boxes of super-sized caterpillars, a bouquet of beautiful butterflies, dozens of feisty fish, and two new friends for my children. That's a miracle worth remembering and a testimony to God's big-hearted nature!

You Can't Out-give God

On another occasion, I took the kids to an arcade and gave each of them a spending allowance of four quarters. I told them that once they had spent all their money, they could not have any more, and we would have to leave.

So off they went from one game to another. As I was watching them, I noticed that my daughter was quick to spend her money, whereas my son was much more careful about it. He began by watching other kids play the games he was interested in and was slow to spend any money. In fact, by the time my daughter had spent all her money, Johnny had yet to spend a single quarter.

When my daughter approached me for more money, I reminded her that she had gotten all she was going to get. So she went to her brother and asked him for a quarter. He refused her and so she came back to me; but I again reminded her that she and her brother had gotten all the money they were going to get and that once he had spent his money, we were going to leave.

When my daughter started getting all worked up, I saw it as an opportunity for my son to be generous. So I suggested that he consider giving his sister a quarter. But he said, "No, this is my money." I agreed with him but still encouraged him to be nice to his sister. He again refused, but after a few moments, he gave in to her whimpering and gave her a quarter.

Tammy spent that quarter just as fast as she had spent the rest of her allowance, and within five minutes she was back asking her brother for more money. This time he told her that there was no way he was going to give her any more and told her to leave him alone. But she persisted until he pushed her away. While she was standing aside pouting, I praised my son for giving her the first quarter, and then gently encouraged him to consider giving her another. Of course, he adamantly refused, saying it wasn't fair. I agreed with him, but I also reminded him that God blesses those who give. He thought about it for a moment and then said, "No way, she's not getting any more of my money!" So I backed off for awhile, and then told him I understood how unfair it was that she kept asking him for money. At the same time, I continued to gently encourage him to be generous.

As I watched him try to decide what to do, I thought to myself, if he gives her any more money, I am going to reward him by taking him to his favorite store so that he can buy anything he wants. Just then, I saw him give his sister another quarter. He then walked over to play a pinball machine. Filled with pride, I cheered him on as he played the three balls the machine allotted him.

Though he did not score very well, the machine started giving him extra balls! So on he went...and despite his continued poor play, the machine kept right on giving him extra balls. I believe he got nine extras in all. When the game had finally ended, I found myself wondering: was that the way the machine worked or was God rewarding him for his generosity?

Well I decided to find out. So I put my own quarter into the machine but only got the expected three balls despite the fact that I scored better than my son. Upon trying it again, I again got only three balls. Then my son played the game again, and he got only three balls. Then we watched several other kids play the game, and they got only three balls. So I thought to myself, can you believe it? I wanted to reward my son by planning a surprise visit to his favorite store, but God beat me to it! He had already returned to Johnny more than three times what he had given his sister. As it is written, there is not one smallest thing we do for one another that God does not reward us for.

Happiness is a Gift From God

As my daughter was growing up, she never wanted me to be out of her sight. Whether she was in the house or out playing with friends, I had to be there with her.

Late one summer, I had planned to spend the weekend with her, but on Saturday afternoon, my brother-in-law invited me to play golf on Sunday morning at an exclusive golf course in the area. As much as I wanted to accept his invitation, there were two problems. The first was that I had planned to spend the day with my daughter; the second was that he was inviting me to play on Sunday—the Sabbath day, which I normally devoted to rest and prayer. But he really wanted me to play and the round had already been paid for. What is more, my sister had invited my daughter to sleep over at her house on Saturday night and would be with her until I had returned from golf on Sunday afternoon. What made the proposition even more tempting was the weather forecast for Sunday—seventies and sunny with light winds and low humidity—the perfect weather for golf!

My sister encouraged me to play, but my daughter seemed to have mixed feelings about it. On the one hand, she wanted me to stay with her, but on the other, she knew she had a friend in my sister. I can still remember Tammy, in her ambivalence, asking me what time I would be back on Sunday.

Even though I knew I was pushing it, I decided to play golf. So my daughter and I slept over at my sister's house. But despite the fact that I was sleeping in a beautiful home with plans to do my favorite thing early in the morning, I could hardly sleep. Something deep inside was telling me that I had made the wrong choice.

As expected, the weather on Sunday was spectacular, and the golf course was in pristine condition. From a logical standpoint, I had it made. Nevertheless, I did not feel that I had God's blessing.

Not surprisingly, things got off to a bad start on the golf course. My opening tee shot went out of bounds, and everything went down hill from there despite the fact that I felt great physically and had had plenty of time to warm up before the round. By the end of nine holes, I was feeling so unhappy that playing golf felt like a burden to me. It was the first time in my life that I had felt like quitting on a beautiful day. By the seventeenth hole I was so miserable and was playing so poorly that I didn't even play the last hole. Interestingly, my poor play was not the problem. It was the other way around—I was playing poorly because I was so miserable.

The miracle in the story is that I had been reminded that happiness is a gift from God. Circumstances don't make us happy, God makes us happy. What makes it so confusing is that we tend to equate happiness with circumstances, when in reality our circumstances are just an outward expression of God's blessings upon us. That is why it is possible to feel unhappy despite favorable circumstances, and happy despite unfavorable ones.

The beauty of nature depends upon God in the same way that our happiness does. Roses are not really red nor are violets really blue. Their "color" is merely the sun's light reflecting off of them. We see the sun's colors in the formation of a rainbow when tiny droplets of water in the air break the sun's light into its component colors. That is also why everything looks grey on a "grey day" until the sun comes out.

So if we want our lives to be rosy red with happiness, we have to seek it from God just as the rose seeks it from the sun. Happiness is not found in what we have or what we are doing any more than a rose's color is found in its stem or its petals. That is what I was reminded of on the golf course that day. I had allowed myself to believe that I had to chase after my happiness rather than remembering that it is a gift that shines down on us from the Father of Lights.

We Plan, God Laughs

It seems that all my life I have been dodging last-minute interruptions and rushing to the first tee whenever I go golfing. So one day I decided to make sure that that didn't happen. I had been invited to play in a golf tournament, which made a timely arrival that much more important. So I decided that I would arrive at the golf course one hour early, which would give me ample time to relax, loosen up, and really play my best.

I was so determined to avoid any interruptions that I literally began making arrangements three months in advance. I began by working it out with my wife, followed by blocking off the entire day in my appointment book and asking one of my colleagues to cover my emergency calls.

The day of the tournament was warm and sunny, and everything went precisely as planned. So I started thinking to myself, I really did it right this time; I covered all my bases. This is what I should do all the time!

Having arrived at the golf course a full hour ahead of our scheduled tee-time, I enjoyed a nice relaxing warm-up and got the tempo of my swing and putting just where I wanted it to be. About five minutes before tee-time, I strolled over to the first tee raring and ready to go. Moments later, the starter turned to our foursome and said, "Fellas, I'm sorry to tell you, but your tee-time has been moved back an hour because the outing in front of you has been moving so slow."

I couldn't believe it. After all that careful planning and preparation, I would have done better had I allowed nature to take its course and arrive at the last minute! The delay meant more than just a loss of time; it meant that much of my preparation would be undone.

The moral of the story is that if you really want something, ask God for it rather than attempting to arrange it all by your self. As our loving Creator, God desires to be a part of our life no matter what we're doing. Then again, there are far too many variables in life to attempt to do things without His help.

Miracle on Father's Day

During the summer of 2005, the weather forecast for Father's Day weekend was spectacular—sunny skies, gentle breezes, low humidity, and temperatures near eighty degrees. Since my father and I love to play golf together, I thought I would invite him to play on Father's Day. Then I got to thinking: I have another father—my Father in heaven. Wouldn't it be nice if I were to spend this Father's Day with Him?

So I changed my plans. I decided that I would give my father a call in the morning and offer to stop by for a little while, but I would spend the rest of the day in prayer and thanksgiving to God for all He does for me.

As I was making these plans, I had been driving to the dealership to drop my car off for some repairs. Knowing that my father would probably invite me to play golf when I called him, I needed a practical excuse not to play. So I decided to leave my golf clubs in my car at the dealership. It would also prevent me from reversing my decision because the dealership would be closed on Sunday and my golf clubs completely inaccessible. Oh how difficult it was to forgo the opportunity to play golf on a beautiful day.

As expected, the weather on Sunday was gorgeous. On my way home from church, I gave my father a call to wish him happy Father's Day. I wasn't surprised when he told me he wanted to play golf. Sadly, I told him I would have loved to but that I did not have my golf clubs with me. I explained that they were in my car, which was having some work done at the dealership. But I told him that I wanted to stop buy and visit. He politely scolded me for leaving my golf clubs in the car, and then invited me over.

When I arrived at his house, he was practically jumping for joy! When I asked him what he was so excited about, he said, "We're going golfing!" "What do you mean," I asked? He said, "I found some golf clubs for you." So I thought to myself, that's wonderful, but he has probably overlooked the fact that I am left-handed. So I said, "That's great, but I think you have forgotten that I'm left-handed." His sassy response was, "I know that."

I was so amazed that he had found left-handed golf clubs on such short notice that there was no way I could refuse him. So I just said, "That's great." But on the inside, I too was jumping for joy as I thanked God for remembering me!

So after a hearty breakfast, we headed out to the golf course. On the way there, we stopped at the home of the friend who had left his clubs for me to use. While my father was getting them, I thought to myself, this is great, but it still won't be like having my own clubs.

When we arrived at the golf course, I was shocked to find that the golf clubs my father found for me were the exact same brand that I use— Ping Eye 2s with square grooves! Not only that, but they felt even better in my hands than my own clubs, and my golf swing felt better than it had ever felt before! What's more, the comfortable temperatures and low humidity made playing in my dressy but casual church clothes feel really nice. In fact, the way I was dressed, I felt like I was playing on the PGA Tour. Then, as if all that were not enough, the starter at the golf course waived us on for free!

So off we went. The clincher was that I played the best golf of my life. I felt loose, relaxed, and hit nearly every fairway and every green— all with the joy of knowing that it was God's gift to me. The take home lesson was that we cannot out-give God; whatever we give to Him, He returns to us in multiples!

A Twist of Fate

While I was swimming at the pool one summer afternoon, I received an urgent message that my son, who was seventeen at the time, had been in a car accident. It was one of those horrifying messages no parent wants to receive. And only a parent can understand what goes through your mind: is he okay? is it serious? is there something I should have warned him about? But for me, the most dreaded thought was that whatever had happened, had happened and could not be undone.

When I hurried upstairs and called about the details, I was told that my son had rented a car with some friends and was driving to Canada when he got into the accident. He had not been injured but had been arrested for drunken driving. My mother, who had taken the emergency call from my son, said he needed for her to send him thirty-eight hundred dollars to bail him out of jail. He begged her not to tell either me or his mother because he feared that we would never forgive him. As an adult and adolescent psychiatrist, that kind of story was all too familiar to me. But I never expected it to hit so close to home.

I was unable to reach his mother, but I was able to contact his grandfather. To my surprise, he told me that my son was actually on the way to the dentist with his mother. He said he would tell my son that I had called and ask him to call me.

I was shocked and confused, but most important, I was pleasantly relieved. When I told my mother the good news, we concluded that someone had probably made a random telephone call and fabricated the story with the intent of getting her to wire the money.

A short time later, my son called to reassure me that he was okay. He went on to tell me not to worry because the whole thing was a miracle. "What do you mean?" I asked. He said he had been working with his grandparents at a church picnic the preceding week and had been placed in charge of the alcohol tent. As he was handing out drinks, he started to ask himself whether there was anything wrong with drinking. He had reasoned to himself that since so many people were drinking at a church function, perhaps it was okay. Yet he remained unsure, and so he had asked God to show him a sign. Ten minutes later, he received the call from his grandfather saying that I was worried about him because I had received a message that he had rented a car with some friends, got into an accident, and been arrested for drunken driving.

My son interpreted this as a clear sign from God that he should not drink. I am sure he was affected even more deeply when he heard me break into tears on the telephone after he had reassured me that he was all right. In His infinite love, God showed my son what his drinking would do to himself and to those who love him. In an amazing twist of fate, He used someone's evil plot to warn my son not to drink, if not for his own good, then for the good of others. As it is written: God has power over good and evil.

Faith and the Healing Power of God's Love

One day I began to notice a hard lump on the side of my knee. The lump was painless, so it concerned me because cancerous lumps normally are painless. X-rays of my knee were normal, and so I scheduled an MRI.

The day before the test, I was out playing with my kids, but I found myself having difficulty giving them my full attention because I was worried about the growth on my knee. So I thought to myself, my worries are distracting me from my children; if I trust in God, I will be freed to love my children, and surely God will return that love to me.

The MRI showed that I had a cracked cartilage in my knee with synovial fluid leaking through the crack and accumulating on the side of the joint. The radiologist found it hard to believe that the injury had not been causing any pain. Yet it wasn't, nor had it ever restricted my athletic activities or range of motion. It was a testimony to the fact that our lives and our abilities are not dependent on our physical condition but on God.

You Can Trust that Small Voice Within

On one occasion, I drove with my family to South Bend, Indiana to visit my wife's sister and attend Easter services with her family. We had arrived on Saturday afternoon after driving all day, and early Sunday morning all eight of us were up bright and early getting dressed for church.

We arrived at the large Greek Orthodox church right on time but were surprised to find that ours was the only car in the parking lot. Naturally, everyone was confused. So the assumption that we had somehow arrived one hour too early. But a small voice in my heart said, "It's okay, just go in." So I told everyone that we should just go into the church. But no one wanted to do that. Instead, everyone wanted go out to breakfast and return in an hour, just in time for the start of services.

Sensing that we were making a mistake by leaving, I considered going into the church by myself. However, I thought it best that all of us stay together. So I went to breakfast with them.

Forty-five minutes later, we arrived back at the church and went in. To everyone's surprise, mass was just ending. Fortunately, we had just enough time to receive Holy Communion. It turned out that we had in fact arrived on time initially but unknowingly had parked in an overflow parking lot in back of the church. Apparently, the main lot had been full the entire time. The experience was a reminder that God speaks to us and that we should trust that small voice within—that small but all-knowing voice of God.

A Biblical Story Relived

During Pentecost, the fifty-day period after the resurrection of Jesus Christ, I had taken the kids fishing at a small pond near our home. We had tried to catch fish there on a few prior occasions but without much luck.

In celebration of the big catch that the apostles enjoyed when the risen Jesus joined them on their fishing boat after the resurrection, I told the kids that they too could expect a big catch. Right from the start, the fish were biting on the worms we were using for bait. But even after we ran out of worms, we continued to catch fish. And not only that, we were catching them left and right. We would just throw our lines in with bare hooks, and a fish would bite every minute or two.

By the third hour, we were catching so many fish that my two children had a contest to see who could catch more fish in ten minutes. I forgot who won, but they each caught about twenty-five fish, and that includes the down time it took to unhook each fish and throw it back into the water. All together, we caught over one hundred and twenty-five fish in just a couple hours. If we had kept an exact count, I would not be surprised if the total was the same number that the apostles caught with Jesus because He was with us too!

Two Missed Opportunities

Several years ago, I woke up early one morning and decided to go golfing since I did not have any patients scheduled until one o'clock in the afternoon. It was a beautiful morning—the sun was shining, the birds were chirping, and the temperature was around seventy-five degrees.

Just as I proceeded to the practice area of the golf course, a small voice within said, "Don't play golf; go to Holy Hill." Holy Hill is a monastery up North where I occasionally went to pray. I thought to myself, what! I don't want to do that now. So for about ten minutes, I went back and forth about it in my mind because I sensed that the Holy Spirit had spoken those words to me. But I had been so intent on playing golf that I talked myself into thinking that perhaps it was just my own self-talk. So I finished warming up and then proceeded to the first tee.

Things had been going okay until I reached the second hole, when I began to notice the excessive humidity. Then, as the sun climbed higher in the sky, it started to get really hot and muggy. By about the fifth hole, I was drenched in sweat. Even my feet were getting wet because there was so much dew on the ground. Worse yet, my hands were perspiring so badly that I was losing my grip when I was swinging at the golf ball. On one shot, the golf club actually slipped out of my hands and went flying into a tree. Fortunately, I was able to retrieve it.

Never in thirty-five years of playing golf had the problem been so bad. By the time I had reached the eighth hole, I hated golf, and I promised myself that I would never again play early in the morning! As I left the golf course, I thought to myself, that's what you get for disobeying God.

On another occasion, a similar thing happened. It was a beautiful day, and I told my wife I would be home late because I was going to play golf after work.

I had been striking the ball beautifully and had a perfect round going when I suddenly heard that small voice within say, "Go home." I thought to myself, what! why now? I had told my wife that I would be home late, and she was fine with it. On the golf course, everything was going great. So why would the Lord want me to leave now?

Unable to decide what to do, I played on. I thought perhaps my disobedience would cause me to start playing poorly, but it didn't; I kept right on playing great. Nevertheless, I could not shake the nagging thought that I should leave.

Then, on the sixth hole, I noticed a line of black clouds beginning to appear over the top of the trees lining the left side of the fairway. I really didn't think much of it because we were playing only nine holes and would finish in plenty of time to avoid the rain. Nevertheless, it kept me thinking. After the next hole, that line of black clouds was covering half the sky. It was at that point that I put two and two together and told the guys I was playing with that I had to go. One of them said, "Wait a minute, you're playing great; you can't leave now!" And the other said, "You're not worried about the rain are you? We have plenty of time to finish." I said, "I know, but I just have to go."

And so I reluctantly began my long walk to the clubhouse. Just as I approached the parking lot, there was a bright flash followed by an earthshaking boom of thunder that served notice that the storm was right over us. Moments later, a torrential rain hit the golf course. In the short time that it took me to cross the parking lot to my car, I was completely drenched.

On my way home, the same voice that had told me to leave the golf course told me to go to a Chinese restaurant where I occasionally ate with my family. Again that didn't make sense because I knew my wife was at home cooking dinner. Nevertheless, I obeyed this time, having learned a lesson from what had just happened.

As I passed by the restaurant, I noticed my wife's car in the parking lot. So I thought to myself, perfect—I'll go in and have dinner with my wife and the kids. But just as I was getting out of the car, they were coming out of the restaurant. When my wife saw me she said, "It's too bad you hadn't come a little sooner because you could have had dinner with us. The kids were talking about you the whole time, wishing you were here."

I then realized how perfect God's counsel and timing had been. Had I left the golf course when He prompted me to, I would have been just in time for dinner and would have avoided the rain, just as I would have avoided the heat had I gone to the Monastery. It made me realize that the God was not trying to rob me of my happiness, He was just trying to help me use my time more productively.

Remember God, and He Will Remember You

When my kids were in grade school, there was always a debate about where we would go and what we would do because my daughter had her own interests and my son had his own. And of course, everything she liked to do was different than what he liked to do.

So early one Saturday morning, we were trying to decide how we would spend the day. My son had a whole list of things he wanted to do, and my daughter had her own list. As we went through the lists, all of us agreed that there was no way we were going to be able to do everything in one day.

Worry turned into panic when I told the kids that we should begin the day by giving thanks to God for all the blessings we had. I suggested that our first activity be to drive up to the Holy Hill Monastery and walk the stations of the cross. At that, they both erupted in protest. "What, no way!" they both exclaimed. "We don't even have enough time to do the things we want to do."

Despite their objections, I explained why it was the right thing for us to do. Not surprisingly, that did not go over very well, so I told the kids to keep in mind that God had the power to extend the length of a day. That caused my daughter to stop and think, but my son wasn't buying it. So I reminded both of them that God created the whole world and that surely He could do a simple thing like hold the sun up in the sky long enough for us to do everything we wanted to do. That sounded convincing to my daughter, but my son remained obstinate. "There's no way," he said. "It's impossible. I'm not going!" Then my daughter joined in: "We never have enough time to do anything we want to do; do we have to go, Papa?" Looking at my son, I said, "I think we should." Then my daughter told her brother with a sigh, "Let's just go, Johnny."

Seeing that my son continued to object, I told the kids that the choice was theirs but that I could not see any way that we were going to be able to do all the things they wanted to do without God's help. With that, my son began to settle down, and then he reluctantly agreed to go to the Monastery.

So off we went on the forty-five minute drive to Holy Hill. We stayed there for about an hour and then drove to the lake where my daughter wanted to go swimming. From that point forward, things went as smooth as silk. We went from one activity to another in what seemed like no time. We avoided traffic jams, we found convenient parking where there normally was none, and most notably, the kids lost no time arguing as we went from one activity to another.

Amazingly, we had gone through both of the kids' wish lists by 6:30 in the evening. The sun was still shining, and there was still plenty of time left in the day, but the kids had had their fill and were content to head home.

As we were going to bed that night, I asked them how we could possibly have done so much in one day, and with so much time left to spare. Both of them agreed that God had rewarded us for starting our day with thanksgiving!

Surrendered to His Love

Many years ago, I had an experience that I am sure most everyone can relate to. Somebody got me mad...I mean really mad!!! Worse yet, I was vacationing with this person on an island, and there was no way I could avoid her! However, I did have some time to be alone, and during that time I contemplated what to do.

I was thinking to myself, I know what I'm gonna do; I'm gonna fix her boots! Just the thought of it gave me a sense of relief. But as I was contemplating how I was going to retaliate, a gentle voice deep inside said, "Don't do that."

But I was so angry at this person that the mere thought of doing nothing drove my blood pressure up and made me even more angry. So I returned to the thought of retaliating. But again the voice said, "Don't do that." So I thought, Lord, I can't just let this go. I know I should, but I just can't; it's simply beyond my capacity. And besides that, she really deserves it!

But the Good Lord kept encouraging me to forgive her. After wrestling with it for awhile, I said, "Lord, if you want to forgive her, you forgive her; but I can't find it within myself to do it!"

Well, I felt the Lord's humble acceptance of that plan, and so when I saw her the next day, I just kept telling myself, I'm gonna stay out of this. I'm just gonna let God do the talking.

When she saw me, she walked up to me, paused for a moment, and to my surprise said, "I'm sorry." Trying to stay out of His way, I just let the Lord respond. After a brief pause, I, or rather He, gently said, "I feel bad about what happened yesterday." She then began to cry and said, "Do you mean you will forgive me?" As I stood there, I could feel the Lord's peace, which led to a gentle smile. She then turned around and started telling everyone what a wonderful person I was. I could not help but overhear the great things she was saying about me. Then I began to think to myself, little does she know that it was not I who forgave her but God. All these great complements are about Him, not me.

The miracle in the story is that I, or rather God, was able to turn this hostile situation into an opportunity for love through forgiveness. That's the miraculous power of God's Spirit!

Two Prayers Answered

My family and I had been vacationing in Phoenix, Arizona and looking at some of the homes in the area—magnificent, high-ceiling, Spanish-style homes up in the mountains. The views through the large picture windows were so spectacular that I felt like I was in paradise.

So I thought to myself, boy, would my mother love to retire in a place like this. Perhaps some day I will have enough money to make that dream come true for her. But as I thought more about it, I began to realize that the area was too isolated. The nearest store was about half an hour away, and the surrounding area was nothing but dry dessert and golf courses. Anyhow, as I continued to look out the window, I said: "Lord, please find a way for me to provide something like this for my mother in a way that would work for her."

About six months later, the administrator at the hospital where I was departmental chairman told me that I needed to attend an upcoming three-day administrative seminar in Fort Lauderdale, Florida. But as it turned out, I had a conflict: I had to fly with my grandmother to New Jersey that week, and so I was excused. The secretary told me that the seminar would be re-offered the following year and that it was really important that I attend. However, the exact date and location had not yet been determined.

When I heard that, I asked God to let it be the one place I had always wanted to go—La Quinta, California. There was a golf course there that I had always dreamed of playing, and what better time to do it than on a mandatory administrative trip?

About nine months later, I was called into the medical staff office and handed an envelope that contained the location and dates for the conference. Remembering my prayer, I carefully looked at the return address in the upper left-hand corner of the envelope. There was a group of small, multicolored palm trees that looked symbolic of Las Vegas, Nevada. I thought to myself, that's close to where I would like to go. I then opened up the envelope and learned that the conference was being held at the Ritz-Carlton Hotel on Frank Sinatra Drive in Rancho Mirage, California, February 5-8. With Las Vegas still on my mind, it took me a few moments to realize that this was the Palm Springs area. Trying to quell the bubbling excitement, I thought to myself, I wonder how far the hotel is from La Quinta? It didn't take me long to find out that it was only ten minutes away! A colleague told me that there were actually two golf courses at the La Quinta Golf Club. He strongly suggested that I play the more scenic Mountain Course. All the while, I kept thinking to myself, what were the odds of this happening? It was like winning the lottery without buying a ticket!

The secretary in the medical staff office told me that I could bring anyone I wished and that all our expenses would be paid. So I thought to myself, my mother loves to lay in the sun as much as I love to play golf, and what could be better than sunny Palm Springs in the middle of a cold Chicago winter? Beyond that, we would be staying at the beautiful Ritz-Carlton Hotel on a street that is named after my mother's favorite singer—Frank Sinatra! Suddenly I realized that this was actually an answer to two different prayers—the one I had said for my mother and the one I had said for myself.

When I told my mother that I had to attend a conference in Palm Springs and that I wanted to take her with me, she thanked me but said there was no way she could come along because she was afraid to fly, especially in the winter. So I just said, "Okay." It did not upset me in the least because I knew beyond a shadow of a doubt that she would be coming. This trip was clearly God's answer to my prayers, and nothing in the world was going to get in the way of it! Trusting in that, I simply told my mother to let me know if she changed her mind.

In the meantime, I proceeded to let the secretary in the medical staff office know that there would be two persons accompanying me—my mother and my step-father. She asked me if I were sure because the airline tickets were nonrefundable. I told her I was. I also started making my mother a cassette tape with all of Frank Sinatra's greatest hits. I can remember hearing his songs being played over and over as I was growing up, and I wanted to play them for her wherever we drove on the trip, beginning with our ride to the airport.

As the date of the conference drew near, my mother inquired about the trip and said that I was lucky to be going to California in the middle of a cold winter. She again said that she wished she could come but that there was just no way. Once again, I accepted her excuse without pressuring her.

About one week before the trip, she said, "You know, I'm just afraid of the snow." Then she said, "I'll tell you what: if there is no snow on the ground the day of the trip, and I see that it is sunny and warm, I'll go." So I thought to myself, yea right, sunny, warm, and no snow on the ground in the middle of a Chicago winter. What are the chances of that happening? About as good as the chances of being sent on a mandatory, all-expenses-paid conference to my favorite place in the world, I thought. In fact, I felt so certain about our being together on the trip that I knew with absolute certainty that I was destined to go on living at least until we had returned from California! It was a sense of assurance that no amount of money or planning could ever provide, and God was arranging it all just for the asking!

A few days before I was scheduled to depart, a warm front came through and melted all the snow on the ground. When I looked out my window on the morning of the trip, the sun was shining brightly with a predicted high of fifty degrees! Not only that, the winds were calm, which meant we would likely have a smooth flight.

It wasn't long before my mother telephoned and said, "I just looked out the window, and it's a beautiful day—I'm coming with you." Well that was no problem for me because I had her ticket ready and had even scheduled the departure for late morning just in case of a last-minute decision.

Needless to say, we had a smooth flight, in fact the smoothest I had ever had. We didn't even feel like we were in an airplane. Upon our arrival at the tiny Palm Springs airport, I gazed through the large picture windows and admired the beautiful palm trees lining the streets and the breathtaking mountains standing like great pyramids in the desert. I found myself wishing that I had planned more than five days.

After we picked up our rental car, I played the Frank Sinatra tape all the way to Frank Sinatra Drive. The winding road up the mountain to the hotel was surrounded by a desert paradise even more beautiful than what I had enjoyed in Scottsdale! For my mother, it was a dream come true because there is nothing she loves more than natural beauty and to lay out in the sun all day. As for me, I spent my first evening on the putting green at the near-by Indian Wells golf course. Early the next morning, my step-father dropped me off at the La Quinta course for an entire day of golf.

I had the time of my life in that mountain paradise. In fact, I played so much golf that I could not straighten up when I got out of bed the next morning. That might sound funny, but honestly speaking, it was a serious problem. In fact, it was so bad that it threatened to ruin the rest of my trip. But rather than allow that to happen, I recognized it as another blessing from God. I knew that there was no way He was going to allow something so ridiculous to interfere with such a meticulously planned trip unless He had something even better in mind.

Realizing that I was not going to be able to play golf for the next few days, I called the McCanns in Los Angeles and invited them to visit us. When I was immediately able to reach Kathleen, and she said they would drive up the following day, I was certain that my injury was God's providence, designed to pull me off the golf course long enough to do something more important. Little did I know that it would be my last opportunity to see one of my greatest mentors, for Dr. McCann would die unexpectedly just a few years later.

I was feeling much better after spending the day with the McCanns and had had the opportunity to play golf again before we returned to Chicago. The Lord had timed everything perfectly.

After five glorious days in the sun, all of us were ready to return home. As you might be expecting by now, our return flight was another perfectly smooth one. The weather in Chicago when we landed was forty degrees under sunny skies with calm winds, and there still wasn't any snow on the ground.

Surprise Trip to Paradise

Eight years after the trip to Palm Springs, I received a call from Kathleen McCann saying that Dr. McCann had died in a drowning accident. The following day I boarded an airplane to Los Angeles. The miracle of the story is that what I thought was going to be a solemn occasion turned out to be the most magical experience of my life.

During the funeral mass and eulogy, I began to sense a gentle tingling throughout my body. It was a sense of spiritual levity that I had never experienced before. The feeling continued into the reception, which was a most unusual sight in itself.

Here we were in a posh community between Bel-Air and Rodeo Drive, gathered together to pay our last respects to a university professor who was one of the pillars of the UCLA dental school, and we were seated at fold-up tables with paper plates and plastic spoons. Of some two hundred guests who attended the funeral, only one was a university professor. The rest were persons from the community of all ages and backgrounds including several minorities and individuals with various handicaps and disabilities. These were the people who Dr. McCann personally helped during his many years in the Westwood community.

The scene reminded me of a passage of Scripture that says, when you throw a party, don't just invite your friends, to whom you have given much and from whom you can expect much; but invite the poor and the homeless, from whom you can expect nothing in return.

If there had been a homeless person there, the biblical scene would have been complete. Just as that thought crossed my mind, I heard someone grunting in the corner of the room. When I looked over that way, I saw a disheveled man wolfing down a plate of food. His hair was covering his entire face, and he was eating like he had never seen food before. I later learned that the man had wandered in off the street, asking for some wine. The woman who greeted him at the door tried to turn him away, but Dr. McCann's wife asked her to let him in because that is what Michael would have wanted. He also would have wanted any cost savings from a humble reception to be used to help those in need, hence the fold-up tables and paper plates.

During the two-hour reception, I heard one person after another talk passionately about the simple but profoundly loving ways in which Dr. McCann had touched their lives. More than one person broke into tears as they told their stories, and I was deeply moved. I am sure that they were equally moved by the stories I shared about the wonderful ways in which Dr. McCann had helped me become a physician.

For three days after I returned home from Los Angeles, I had remained filled with a freedom of spirit that made all the cares of this world seem frivolous. The best way I can describe it is that my soul had been taken up to heaven. On more than one occasion, I mistakenly told those who asked me where I had gone that I had attended a wedding!

You Can Trust in God

For the past twenty years, my two uncles, my cousin, and I have been playing a yearly golf tournament. It's a long tradition in which all of us look forward to competing for a family trophy.

A few years back, my uncle called and said he could come to Chicago for a four-day tournament any one of the upcoming three weekends. The choice of weekend would be crucial because in Chicago, it's hard to find one day in which the weather is permitting, let alone four days in a row. What we did have going for us was that we were in the middle of a drought and had seen scarcely a drop of rain in nearly a month. Logically, we thought the time to do it would be as soon as possible, before the drought ended. But without the benefit of a forecast, I turned to God for guidance.

My petition to God was met by a small voice in my heart that said, "Don't do it this weekend; do it the following weekend." When I suggested this to the guys, they all thought it was a bad idea because the rain was sure to come sooner or later, and they thought we should strike the iron while it was hot and schedule the tournament for the upcoming weekend. Surprisingly, they still allowed me to make the final decision.

The first part of the miracle is that the weekend I had suggested that we skip turned out to be terrible. It was hot and humid, with temperatures near one hundred degrees and thirty to forty mile-per-hour winds—not your ideal conditions for playing golf. That was followed by a stretch of five days during which it rained or drizzled almost continuously. As we approached the end of the week, things were not looking good. My uncle was scheduled to arrive on Saturday at noon, just a few hours before our scheduled tee time. It continued to rain right through Friday, and when I looked out the window on Saturday morning, it was still raining!

At around 11:30 Saturday morning, the rain finally stopped, and at noon, when we picked my uncle up from the airport, we saw the first break in the clouds in nearly a week. When we arrived at the golf course at 3:00 p.m., the temperature was seventy-five degrees and there was not a cloud in the sky!

The weather continued to be sunny and mild for the next four days, with highs in the upper seventies and lower eighties—ideal for golf. We played each of those days, and it was actually the first time in two decades that we played four consecutive rounds. The experience was just another reminder of God's faithfulness and the intimacy that He desires to have with us.

Don't Forget God

Although we can trust in God, we must be careful not to forget God in our pursuit of pleasure and pastime. On another occasion, the guys wanted to play golf on Sunday. Deep inside I did not feel that we should because it was the Sabbath day, but I was torn between honoring God in my usual way, which involves resting and reflecting on His word, and playing golf with my family during my uncle's visit to Chicago.

Although the guys sensed that I had some reservations about playing golf on Sunday, they really wanted me to come. So not wanting to spoil the party, I decided to go with them.

We had signed up for eighteen holes, but on the ninth, my cousin became so angry about his poor play that he threw one of his golf clubs over the fence into someone's yard. The problem with retrieving it was that the fence was too high to climb, and there was no one on the other side to return it to him. Of course, that made him even more angry, particularly because it was a brand new club. The combination of his anger and his need to retrieve his golf club was enough to cause us to quit after only nine holes. So instead of finishing the round that all of us had paid for, we wound up driving around the neighborhood looking for my cousin's golf club. It wasn't what we wanted to do, but we nevertheless found ourselves doing it. That is the kind of thing that happens when we do things that are not seasoned with God's blessings.

Honesty is the Best Policy

Several years ago, I was out on a drive with my teen-aged cousin when he asked me if he could drive for a bit. He told me he had a driver's permit and needed to get some practice in before taking his driver's test.

Seeing that we were just a half block from home, I pulled over and exchanged seats with him. Excited to be behind the wheel, he stepped on the accelerator and tried to race around the narrow turn into our condominium complex. Well, he didn't turn sharply enough and crashed headlong into the light-pole on the median strip. The forty-foot pole came crashing down over the hood of the car and cracked into pieces when it hit the pavement. With my radiator shooting water up from under the smashed hood and the shattered light-pole laying across the road, I calmly asked Mark to trade places with me. "You mean you're not mad at me?" he asked. Again I said to him, "Just get out of the car and trade places with me." So both of us got out and traded places. I then backed the car up and slowly drove the short distance to our parking lot.

As I pulled into a parking space, two squad cars pulled up behind us. A female officer approached and asked me to step out of the car. Before I could say anything, she started performing sobriety tests on me. Meanwhile, I started wondering what I should say. These officers were under the impression that I was the one who had crashed the car, and my first instinct was to say nothing in order to protect my cousin. But as I thought about it further, I realized that to say nothing would be to deceive the police, which would be the same as lying. Yet I dreaded the thought of letting my cousin be ticketed before he even had a driver's license. I imagined his driving privileges being withheld for many years and dreaded what the girls would think of a guy who was in his twenties and still unable to drive? I also thought about the trouble he would be in with his parents and the shame that this thing would bring upon him for years to come. But while everything in my logical mind was telling me to say nothing, my moral mind was telling me that honesty was the best policy.

Unable to decide what to do, I interrupted the officer who was examining me and said, "Officer, I have a problem." "What is your problem?" she asked. I said, "I'm really not sure what to do. You see, my cousin was driving the car when we hit the pole. But before you arrived, we traded places and I drove into the parking lot. Now you're under the assumption that I did it, and I don't want to put my cousin in trouble. So I'm not sure what to do." The officer's response was, "Sir, you've done the right thing." Then all four police officers abruptly left me and went to question my cousin. I felt so small and unfaithful as I stood there by myself watching the police begin to interrogate my cousin.

After the officers had finished questioning him, they took us down to the police station, where I learned that my cousin had not even had a driver's permit! He had lied about it just to get me to let him drive my car. Of course, my cousin was ticketed, and we were given a court date.

I had not heard from my cousin until about three weeks later, when we appeared in court together. Not having any experience with such matters, we had no attorney and just prepared ourselves for the worst. As we stood waiting for judgment to be pronounced, the district attorney stepped over to me and gently said, "Your case is dismissed; the two of you and can exit out that door." My cousin and I could't believe it!

But that was not the end of the matter. When the bill came for the light-pole, my cousin's father reamed me out for "opening my big mouth" and telling the police that his son had been in the driver's seat. He was mainly upset about the fact that he was responsible for replacing the three-thousand-dollar light-pole, which, according to him, would have been covered under my automobile insurance policy had I allowed the police to assume that I had been the driver. Well what could I say? I just felt really bad about the whole thing.

But several days later, I received a call from my insurance adjuster telling me that the company was going to pay for the light-pole. When I asked why, he said that my car had liability insurance regardless of who was behind the wheel. He also told me that there would not be an increase in my insurance rates since I had not been the driver. He just asked me not to let anyone drive my car again.

Sometime later, I saw my cousin and his father. "How did you know?" his father asked me. "Know what?" I asked. "Know that everything was going to work out?" he said. Humbled by the whole thing, I simply said, "I didn't; I just thought I needed to tell the truth." "Well," he said, "we will never question you again."

Twenty-five years have passed, and my cousin tells me that he is such a safe driver that he has rarely even gotten a traffic ticket. He says that his safe driving is the direct result of what happened that night that he crashed into the light-pole.

So simple honesty got my cousin's traffic ticket dismissed, it got the light-pole and my car repaired without raising my insurance rates, and most important, it taught my cousin a life-long lesson in driver's safety. That's the power of the truth! God is that very truth, and where the truth is, so too is He and His helping hand.

He Who Honors God Will Be Honored

Many years ago, I was vacationing with my family during Lent and had attended church services in a newly developing Christian community in Scottsdale, Arizona. The service was being held in what was the equivalent of a tent, and a collection was taken up for the completion of the church. Considering the condition of the make-shift church where we were celebrating Mass, I simply could not see myself spending hundreds of dollars on golf while the house of God was in such disarray. So I dropped my golf allowance into the church collection basket.

When my wife found out what I had done, she scolded me for giving away all my money and said that there would be no golf for me. I felt bad about it but did not want to argue with her. Given that it was the Lenten season, I was not convinced that playing golf was the right thing for me to be doing anyway.

Two days later, my wife told me that her mother, who had been vacationing with us, had purchased for me a nonrefundable golf pass to the TPC (Tournament Player's Club) of Scottsdale. Her generous gift turned my sadness into joy! The fact that the pass was nonrefundable told me that God wanted me to play, and it was at one of my favorite golf courses!!! I interpreted it as a sign that God had remembered me just as I had remembered Him.

The following year, we were again vacationing in Scottsdale during Lent and were with three of my best friends-three older doctors with whom I really enjoyed playing golf. Normally when I played golf with them, I would focus on my own game in an effort to impress them—something that I really had fun doing as the youngest and most experienced golfer of the group. But on that day, I decided to make a Lenten sacrifice by devoting myself to helping one of the guys really improve his game. So rather than focusing on my game on the practice range, I watched Andy hit balls. To his delight, we focused exclusively on his swing and his game in preparation for the round.

Even after we teed off, I remained more attentive to Andy's game than mine. I did not fully appreciate how much of an effort I had been making on his behalf until the eleventh hole, when I was so focused on his game that I forgot to hit my own tee shot!

When all was said and done, Andy turned in the best score of his life, topping his previous best by twenty strokes! He told me that it was one of the happiest days of his life and asked me to do him the honor of allowing him to pay for my round. I smiled and told him I was so happy for him that I felt like I had topped my own best score, despite the fact that I really hadn't played very well at all.

About a month later, there was a wedding in the family, and several of the guys were talking shop. I could not help but overhear Andy telling everyone what a great golfer I was. I could not understand why he was saying that because that last time we had played together, I played terrible. Then I began to realize that it was not so much my talent that he was bragging about but my generosity. It has been said that people forget what you say and do, but they never forget how you make them feel. This was certainly an example of that. But the miracle of the story is that in my effort to make a sacrifice for God by devoting myself to another person, I wound up accomplishing the very thing I thought I was sacrificing—my desire to impress the guys. In my effort to honor God, He had honored me.

Two Prayers for My Daughter

Last year my daughter needed some dental work and asked for my help. So I did my best to find a quality dentist in her area. Not knowing anyone personally, I did what most people would do nowadays and read the reviews on a number of local dentists. One dentist had a five-star rating based on over five hundred reviews, so I sent Tammy to her.

At the appointment, the dentist asked Tammy who her previous dentist was, citing the poor quality of her work. She then proceeded to refill two of Tammy's teeth. When I asked Tammy how she liked her new dentist, she said that she seemed very knowledgeable and confident but was difficult to talk to. Tammy said she felt too intimidated to ask the doctor any questions. That really got my attention because my daughter is not a shy person.

Knowing from experience the folly of pride and that such individuals fail to learn as much as they fail to listen, I told Tammy that I wanted to find her a different dentist. Though she could not comprehend the logic of my quick assessment, she agreed to postpone any further work with that dentist until I found another.

Having concluded that good reviews were not a guarantee of good service, I turned to God for help. In all humility, I asked Him to help me find a quality dentist for my daughter. Praise be to our Lord, the next dentist I found was just that; she was so humble that she came to the phone even though all I wanted was to talk to her secretary. When I explained the situation with Tammy, she told me that she really wanted to get her in right away but that her afternoon was tied up with some complex problems that an elderly patient was having. When I considered the amount of time she had set aside for the other patient, I knew that I had found the right dentist for my daughter.

When Tammy asked how I had made my decision, I explained that just as pride blinds a person, humility gives them sight. Indeed, after evaluating Tammy, the new dentist was concerned that the fillings the other dentist had just done might need to be redone. Although that was no different than what the previous dentist had said about the work of Tammy's first dentist, it was the humility with which she said it that reassured me that she knew what she was talking about.

After several visits, Tammy found the new dentist to be thorough, compassionate, and flexible. She was made to feel that she could ask any question and that she could call the doctor at any time. In an effort to save Tammy's teeth, Dr. Johnson was also willing to make exceptions for Tammy, including seeing her on weekends if necessary. After several months of treatment, Tammy began to see Dr. Johnson as more than just a trusted dentist; she was getting to see her as caring friend and role model as well.

Not long after that, Tammy happened to call me while I was praying at a grotto of the blessed Virgin Mary. During the conversation, we got to talking about how great it was that her brother Johnny had just been accepted to law school. Though older than Johnny, Tammy was still very much in limbo about her career plans; nothing really seemed to interest her. Sensing that she saw Johnny as being in an enviable position, I reminded her that it was not only Johnny's hard work but also my constant prayers and trust in God that had gotten him into law school. That having been said, I told her that I would pray for her too and ask our blessed Lady to help her find her career. As I turned my attention to Virgin Mary, I heard her speak to my heart and tell me how full of joy she was that I was bringing Tammy's needs to her.

Just three weeks later, Tammy called me with some exciting news. She told me that she had decided to become a nurse practitioner. What she liked about it was that she would be able to prescribe medication without having to go through all the work of becoming a physician. Although this in itself might not sound like a miracle, it takes on new meaning when you consider two things: first that Tammy had for years been indecisive about what she wanted to do with her life; and second that her father is a pioneer in the treatment of mood disorders. I explained to her that under normal circumstances she would be at a disadvantage because she would be competing with medical doctors. However, were she to specialize in the area of mental health, she would be able to use my knowledge and experience to become competitive with any doctor in the area, including any psychiatrist.

By God's grace, she immediately recognized the wisdom of what I was saying and reminded me that her undergraduate degree was in psychology. She then told me that she had been working on her plan for about three weeks and that she had just finished working out all the details. As I reflected on the timing of it, I realized that God must have given her the idea immediately after I brought my petition to Our Lady. Beyond giving her a wonderful career, her area of practice would open the door to a lifetime of collaboration between the two of us as I work to impart my knowledge to her for the benefit of her patients. It would also be the gateway to a wide range of spiritual discussions as I help Tammy to help her patients in a holistic way. Little did I know that the books I have written on spirituality, mood disorders, and chronic pain were to become instruction manuals for my daughter in the promising new career God had given her in answer to my prayer!

The grotto where I prayed for Tammy

God's Amazing Providence

My grandmother just turned ninety-three, and I am her primary caretaker. She has a history of mild diabetes but is otherwise in excellent health. She had been caring for herself independently until four years ago when she started to have so much trouble walking that she began to need daily assistance.

Because of bad experiences in the hospital, she is opposed to seeing doctors and insists that she would not live more than three days in a nursing home. So she has been insistent on remaining in her home regardless of the circumstances. Of course, we too want to see her remain in her home if possible, so her son takes her shopping once a week, and I have adjusted my schedule so that I do not have to leave her for more than four or five hours at a time. For me, the biggest sacrifice was that I could no longer play golf whenever I wanted. For awhile I tried, but between my professional responsibilities and my increasing concerns about my grandmother falling at home alone, I eventually came to the realization that I would have to put my life on hold for awhile.

Just as the frustration of caring for my grandmother was beginning to erode my relationship with her, I developed sciatica that eventually became so debilitating that I could barely walk. The miracle is that my condition slowed me down to my grandmother's pace and made me much more patient and empathic. It also prevented me from doing very much outside the home, which in turn made taking care of my grandmother feel more like an opportunity than a burden. Consequently, I began to enjoy my time with her and naturally became more available to her. We would sit and talk about her life, and she would give me advice about mine. We would also listen to old songs and watch movies that brought back fond memories of her past. Seeing that she was drawing close to the end of her life, and I needed to strengthen my faith to overcome my illness, I generally chose biblical and other inspirational movies for us to watch. As time went on, what I originally experienced as a sacrifice for her became a kind of spiritual retreat for me. After a few years, I began to realize that she was living more for me than I for her.

As if to accommodate this, my new patient referrals gradually diminished, and my psychiatric practice mysteriously became very quiet—even more quiet than in my first year of practice. The down time also gave me the opportunity to incorporate new spiritual insights into my book "Images of Heaven," and it allowed me to write this book "Miracles," a book that I had for many years been wanting to write but which I had postponed because of my busy schedule.

My illness also allowed me to see things from the patient's perspective—an experience that has benefited my patients enormously. Albert Schweitzer once said that a physician does not develop true compassion and desire to serve the sick until he has been sick himself. I can certainly attest to that. Moreover, my struggle with illness has given me insights into the practice of medicine that no amount of schooling or clinical experience could have given me.

It has also been said that it is in dying that we learn to live. Being laid up like this has given me a real understanding of what that means. When my symptoms first began, I had the sense that I would never completely regain my physical health. The experience brought me face to face with my mortality and allowed me to see that I had in many ways been selling my soul to the devil in exchange for the pleasures of this world. Over time, my physical limitations have had the effect of uprooting pride, selfishness, gluttony, avariciousness, unjustness, disobedience, self-neglect, and all the other sins that prevent a person from truly living.

But the specific malady with which I am struggling has targeted my pride more than anything else. I went from being a healthy, strong, self-opinionated person to someone who walks with a cane, cannot lift a plate, and constantly needs to rely on others for help. It is a problem perfectly suited to my spiritual needs because it has taught me that the only way I am going to recover is through patience, faith, and the practice of all the other virtues. When my initial attempts at a quick fix through modern medicine repeatedly failed, I began to realize that God was allowing me to remain in my debilitated state for as long as it took for my attitude to change and my soul to be cleansed.

The providential nature of the illness was affirmed by a strange accident that occurred after an excellent chiropractor got me so much improvement that I started to think that my spiritual retreat was over and that I could go back to doing whatever I wanted to do, including playing golf. But while I was having fantasies about getting back on the links, I had forgotten something that a small voice inside had told me when my grandmother lost her ability to walk independently. The voice had said that if I just stayed focused on caring for my grandmother, I would surely be back to playing golf when the job was done.

Anyhow, I had actually been on my way to the golf course for the first time in two years when I stopped at Walgreens to pick up some medicine for my grandmother. As I was exiting the parking lot, I came to a stop behind a large truck that was waiting to exit in front of me. As I was waiting for the driver to make his turn, he suddenly began to back up into me! I reflexively shouted "no!!!" and tried to throw my car into reverse. But it was too late—he plowed right into me, crushing the front end of my car and jarring my body just enough to undo all the progress I had made through months of therapy with the chiropractor.

I couldn't believe what had happened. So the other driver and I got out to asses the damages. He said he was backing into a loading dock and didn't see me. In any case, his truck was fine, but my front end had significant damage. Even so, I was still intent on getting to the golf course. I just figured that we would exchange insurance information and be on our way.

But when I attempted to park my car, I noticed that the left front tire was rubbing against the frame just enough to make the car undrivable. So I was forced to call a tow truck. Thus, all my plans for golf were busted by this freak accident. What is more, my golf clubs were towed away with my car. That meant I couldn't even go golfing using my other car.

Well, I got the message: NO GOLF NOW. The close timing between my idea of returning to golf and the freak accident that not only kept me from getting to the golf course but also re-injured me and took my golf clubs away drove home the message that I was to stay focused on caring for my grandmother.

To most people, this story might sound a bit trite. But the good Lord knows how passionate I am about golf and how difficult it would be for me to have the opportunity to play but be unable to because of the ongoing responsibility of caring for my grandmother. So God has kept me where I am safest—where I am physically unable to play. My physical limitations keep me caring for my grandmother graciously rather than begrudgingly, and that makes all the difference because she is very sensitive.

Through the accident, God showed me His providence in yet another way. The policeman who had arrived to make out the report asked me if I would be needing a ride anywhere. I had actually been planning to see a patient after I stopped at the golf course, and I was beginning to realize that I was getting late for that appointment. So the policeman offered to drive me to work even before he was done making out his report. He asked the person who hit me to wait at the scene while he dropped me off at my office. He then went back and finished the report, after which he returned to my office with my license and a copy of the completed report. I really got the royal treatment! I was also fortunate to have been driving my old car because I had been thinking about selling it anyway. As it turned out, the cost of the repair exceeded the value of the car, so I spent a small portion of the insurance reimbursement on a limited repair and sold the car at a reduced price, which benefited both the buyer and me. It was all God's way of telling me that what had happened was meant for my good and not my harm.

As time goes on, I find myself being able to see more and more clearly how God is using my down time to help me even as I am helping my grandmother. Most importantly, I have come to see how my pride had been hampering my ability to reach my full potential. This experience has taught me to ask for help and work together with others rather than continue to be self-reliant and competitive. It has also reminded me that without God's help, I cannot do anything good.

So important are the lessons I have learned that on at least one occasion, they have enabled me to save my grandmother's life. The incident about which I am thinking began with the purchase of an intercom system that for safety reasons I had installed in my grandmother's bedroom. A few months after I installed it, I was awoken by a stirring of the covers in my grandmother's bedroom. When I got up to check on her, she appeared to be in a kind of daze. She was able to answer my questions appropriately, but she was looking off into space rather than at me. She also kept repeating herself.

Because it was so early in the morning, I thought perhaps it was just a sleep phenomenon. Anyhow, I normally would have tried to handle the whole thing myself, especially because I am a physician. But having learned, through my physical weakness, to reach out to others for help, I told my grandmother that I wanted to call her children.

When I called her daughter (my mother), she told me to call 911. Being a doctor myself, I was not very inclined to do that in the absence of convincing evidence that there was a medical emergency. Furthermore, my grandmother had previously made me promise never to force her to go to the hospital. She had repeatedly been telling me that she wanted to die in her home. She had even put it in writing. But seeking to obey my mother, I hung up and called emergency services.

The Paramedics arrived in less than five minutes, and after asking a few questions, checked my grandmother's blood sugar. I had not thought to do that despite the fact that she had been on medication for mild diabetes because upon prior testing, her blood sugar had never been low. But surprisingly, when the paramedics checked it, it was not only low, it was dangerously low! They immediately gave her glucose intravenously, and within less than a minute, she was back to normal.

As expected, she threw a fit when she saw the paramedics standing around for bed. She demanded to know who had let them in and refused to go to the hospital. So the paramedics asked her to sign a form documenting that she was refusing medical advice. I told her that they had saved her life, but she argued with me, saying that there had been nothing wrong with her and that I should never have called them or allowed them into her apartment.

My new-found humility had not only given me the wisdom and willingness to obey my mother and call 911 but it had also allowed me to accept blame from my grandmother without getting defensive. She might never understand that she could have gone into a coma and suffered brain damage or possibly even death, but I did not allow that to stop me from thanking my mother and my Lord for helping me save her from that.

Not surprisingly, my grandmother also refused to see her doctor about the low blood sugar, and so in consultation with one of my colleagues, I had her stop taking the medication she had been on for diabetes. Fortunately, she has not had any episodes of hypoglycemia since that time.

Looking back on it, I never would have thought that I could call the paramedics and have them treat my grandmother for a life-threatening condition without her having to go to the hospital. But those are the kind of miracles that are made possible when one acts humbly and cooperatively, as the Lord taught by His own example. And just as He was brought back to life through His obedience to His Father, my grandmother was brought back to life through my obedience to my mother.

Through this experience, God demonstrated His love and integrity in yet another way. You see, my grandmother insists that doctors cannot help her and that God is her only doctor. So God honored her faith without dishonoring His own methods. He sent his instruments—the paramedics—while she was unconscious. Back when I was contemplating becoming a doctor, I asked a hospital chaplain why doctors were necessary even for those who have faith. He said, "The Lord has many instruments, and sometimes He uses doctors and nurses in the healing process." Fr. Traynor's simple explanation allowed me to finalize my decision to become a physician and was certainly affirmed by this experience with my grandmother.

Faith: More Than Positive Thinking

A few years ago I had taken my grandmother to the dentist in her car, and on our way back home, she had asked me to stop for gas. So I pulled into a 7-Eleven and filled her tank. But when I got back into the car, it would not start. I kept turning the key, but there was no response at all. I told my grandmother that we would have to call a tow truck.

Afraid to let me do that, she told me to ask someone for help. I told her that no one could help us because we were at a 7-Eleven, not a service station. Nevertheless, she insisted that I ask for help without towing the car. So just to please her, I asked a young man who was putting gas in his car if he could help us. He looked at me like a deer in the headlights, shook his head, and quickly got back into his car. Then I went into the 7-Eleven, where the only attendant was a woman who was busy serving a line of customers. Again to appease my grandmother, I interrupted to tell the attendant what had happen, and she told me that I needed to push my car away from the pump so that other patrons could get gas. That added insult to injury because I had recently hurt my back and was unable to push the car.

So my grandmother said that we needed to call her son because he was the one who took care of her car. But then she remembered that he had just started a new job, and she did not want to interrupt him. That was when I decided that I really needed God's help. What came to mind was a passage of scripture that says God's strength is perfected in our weakness. With that, I asked God to bail me out of the situation.

So I again tried to start the car; but it still wouldn't start. As I continued to pray, I kept trying to start the car; but there was absolutely no response. Still, I kept praying and turning the key, but nothing happened. After about five minutes of this, my grandmother said, "What are you doing? Can't you see that it won't start?" I said to her, "Don't worry, it will start." So I kept turning the key despite the fact that the car was completely dead. After another five minutes and about one hundred more turns of the starter mechanism, I began to think, Lord, this is the first time you have ever let me down. Yet even as that thought was crossing my mind, I was continuing to turn the starter mechanism and suddenly boom—the car started right up as if nothing was wrong with it. In my excitement, I felt the Lord say, "I caught you doubting Me." After that, I promised God and myself that I would never doubt Him again.

When my grandmother told her son what had happened, he said that a similar thing had happened before with the car. But I said, "No, I think God fixed the car for us." His reply was, "Yea right, now God is a mechanic." Then he said he would have to take the car in to have it checked out. My response was, "Okay, but don't be surprised if they can't find anything wrong with it."

As it turned out, many months passed before my uncle had a chance to take the car in to be serviced, and yet the problem never recurred. He did eventually take the car in, but the mechanic could not find anything wrong with it.

The Power of Faith

As I shared in a previous memoir, I am my grandmother's primary caretaker. I do things like take her to the dentist, help her to the bathroom, and prepare her meals. A fussy eater to begin with, she almost completely stopped eating after the last two teeth in her mouth were pulled a few years back. Although the teeth had been replaced by a new denture, she could not chew very well. At that point, one of the few foods of substance that she continued to be willing and able to eat was a Middle Eastern dish called Hareesah.

Because she prefers the way they prepare it at our community Church, she had been asking me to bring some home for her after Sunday services. The problem was that I never knew when the church was going to make it. The other problem was that many people make their way downstairs to the meeting hall before church services have ended, and the Hareesah is often sold out by the time I get there.

During one stretch of time, my grandmother had been waiting over six weeks for some Hareesah. As I was standing during final prayers that Sunday, I began to debate whether to leave church (before the Hareesah was sold out) or finish my prayers and trust in God for the Hareesah.

Actually, I was contending with two potential problems: the food could be sold out, but it was also possible that the women hadn't even cooked Hareesah that day. So even if hurrying downstairs would circumvent the first problem, it was not going to help if the ladies had not cooked the food that day. In any case, I decided to rely upon God for the food and finish my prayers before going downstairs.

After church had ended, I arrived downstairs only to find that they had not even cooked Hareesah. Still trusting in God for the food my grandmother wanted so badly, I just stood there at the service counter. Then something very unusual happened. One of the ladies whispered to me that they had some Hareesah in the refrigerator from a previous day. So she went and got it for me, asking me not to tell anyone.

There are three ways in which faith worked its magic here. The first is that it led me to ask for Hareesah even though it had been obvious from the empty cooking vats that it had not been made that day. The second is that one of the cooks was willing to go out of her way and get me the leftovers from the cooler. And the third is that they even had any to offer me because it is usually sold out!

The following week at church, I was faced with the same question: should I head downstairs early, or should I again rely on God? This time I reasoned to myself that if the ladies had not cooked the Hareesah, my faith was not going to make any difference. Either they had cooked it or they hadn't. And if they had not cooked it, what were the chances of another lucky break like the one the previous week?

Trampling my reasoning under the foot of my faith, I finished my prayers in church, reminding myself that just as God came through for me the previous week, He could do it again.

The first thing I noticed when I arrived at the service counter downstairs was that once again, they had not cooked Hareesah. Trying not to lose faith, I just stood there as the ladies busily went about serving other foods to the parishioners. Then suddenly, a lady who I had never met before walked up to me and told me that she and her daughter were cooking Hareesah at home for my grandmother! She told me that her daughter was presently getting it ready and wanted to know when she could bring it to my grandmother's house. I couldn't believe my ears! So I told the woman the whole story and how I had been praying that God would provide this favorite food for my grandmother.

Sure enough, the woman and her daughter arrived at my grandmother's apartment early that evening and dropped off enough fresh-cooked Hareesah for our whole family!

Don't Doubt God

During the third year of caring for my grandmother, I received a summons for jury duty. When I received the letter, I thought to myself, I can't do this because I have to take care of my grandmother. Not only that, I can't do all that walking and sitting with this problem I'm having with my leg and back. So I began to wonder, how am I going to tell the State that I, as a practicing physician, cannot perform my civic duty? Or how can I claim that I can barely walk due to sciatica, when I am both working and caring for my grandmother? The whole thing would sound like a grand excuse to get out of jury duty.

So I really knew I was going to need God's help. When I humbly asked the Lord to help me, His response was, "Don't worry, you won't have to go. But they won't excuse you until the last minute." So I decided to deal with it by simply telling the Jury Commissioner that I was my grandmother's primary caretaker and that I could not leave her for an extended period of time.

When the Jury Room Supervisor heard my explanation, she said I would need a doctor's verification. So I asked my grandmother's dentist, the only doctor she had seen in recent years, if he would write a letter attesting to the fact that my grandmother was unable to walk independently and that I was her primary caregiver. I felt that it was a fair request because he had on several occasions seen me assist her to his office. He agreed to write the letter, and about two weeks prior to my jury date, I faxed the letter to the Jury Room Supervisor along with a written explanation of my circumstances. In my letter, I asked the supervisor to contact me or my grandmother if there were any questions.

When I did not hear back from anyone in scheduling, I assumed that I had been excused. By the time my jury date arrived, I felt so sure that I had been excused that I started to question the accuracy of what I thought God had told me in my heart—that they would not excuse me until the last hair-raising minute.

Then, two days after my jury date, I received a letter stating that I had not been excused and that I was expected to appear as originally scheduled. So I thought to myself, oh that's just great; now I have failed to appear! So I immediately called the Jury Room Supervisor, who told me there was no way I could be excused without a note from a physician. The letter from the dentist had been insufficient. So we wound up getting into a long telephone discussion in which she just could not understand how I, as a physician, was my grandmother's primary caregiver nor could she understand how I could not produce a letter from a physician, as opposed to a dentist, regarding my grandmother's inability to walk.

So I just kept telling her the truth and praying that she would understand. Nevertheless, she refused to believe my story, and so I had no choice but to accept it. Well having accepted "no" as her final answer, I offered to let her speak with my grandmother, just to show her that I had been telling her the truth. Then she said, "Oh that's okay. But I'll tell you what: I'll give you a six month deferral."

I couldn't believe it! What a dramatic turn of events. Not only was I relieved, but I thought to myself, when God says not until the last minute, He really means it!!!

But that's not the end of the story. Six months later, I received another jury summons. Fortunately, the same supervisor gave me another extension. After another six months, I received yet another extension. As grateful as I was, I began to think that sooner or later my request for extensions was going to be denied. So when they called me again for what was the fourth time, I again turned to God for help. This time He simply told me that everything would be fine and that I would be excused again.

So I confidently placed a call to the Jury Room Supervisor to explain that I was still caring for my grandmother. She had been unavailable when I called, and her partner insisted upon helping me herself. After I began to explain my situation, she asked me how many times in the past my jury appearance had been deferred. When I told her two or three, she said that the department normally only permitted one six-month deferral. When I explained that the supervisor was familiar with the unusual nature of my circumstances, she said that she would have her call me back. So I left her two contact numbers: my cellular phone and my home phone, thinking that if she chose to call the house, she would have a chance to speak to my grandmother.

Early the next morning, the home phone rang, but when I picked it up, I accidentally pressed the disconnect button and lost the call. As I thought about who might have called so early in the morning, it occurred to me that it might have been the Jury Room Supervisor. Anticipating that she might call back, I quickly began to rehearse what I was going to say. As I was thinking about it, an idea came to mind: I thought I would tell her that the reason no one could care for my grandmother in my absence was that the job required a great deal of patience, the kind of patience that I alone have had because I can barely walk myself due to sciatica.

Until then, I had been reluctant to use my own trouble walking as an excuse because I thought that if they denied my request or my walking improved, it would then be hard to go back and explain that I still had to care for my grandmother. It would just sound too far-fetched, particularly because I had previously told the supervisor that I had still been seeing patients as a physician.

Just after I had finished planning my explanation, the Jury Room Supervisor called me on the alternative number I had provided. She said she had called earlier but that someone had answered and then hung up. She apologized for the delay in calling me at my alternative number but said that she had been interrupted. When I explained the situation just as I had mapped out, she told me that there was no way she could give me another deferment. But since I had explained at the start of our conversation that it was my own difficulty walking that was allowing me to have the patience to care for my grandmother, I was in position to use it as an alternative excuse when she denied my request for a fourth extension. So I said, "I have an idea that might help us out. I am currently seeing the Chiropractor three times a week for my sciatica. The problem started at precisely the time that my grandmother lost her ability to walk independently, as if God was forcing me to slow down and be patient with her." I told her that if it weren't for that, the frustration of caring for her would likely cause my grandmother, who hates to depend on people, to try to walk by herself and fall. "So," I said, "How about if this time I ask my doctor to write a letter on my behalf? I have an appointment with him today. And if my grandmother still needs me when I get better, we'll deal with it then." She said, "That's a good idea. We would prefer that the letter be from a physician, but I will accept it from your Chiropractor."

When I called the doctor's office to request the letter, he had it ready for me when I arrived. So it was fortuitous that I had missed the supervisor's wake-up call and equally fortuitous that she had not tried to reach me at my alternative number until after I had organized my explanation.

I believe that God had intervened to help me in at least three ways. First, I believe He caused me to accidentally disconnect the telephone when I was still half asleep and unprepared to talk. Second, I believe He gave me the clever idea of weaving my difficulty walking into the story by connecting it to my patience with my grandmother before my request for another deferment had been denied. Third, I believe He caused the supervisor to delay calling me at the alternative number until I had organized the plan He had given me.

A Double Miracle

About one year after my grandmother's last two remaining teeth were removed and a new denture was placed, she started to have severe pain in an area underneath the denture. When I discuss the problem with her dentist, he said that it was probably caused by the potato chips she had recently started eating. He said that chip fragments were likely irritating the skin underneath the denture.

When I told my grandmother this, she disagreed even though she herself was the first to suspect the chips. She argued that it could not have been the chips because she had been eating them on the side opposite the painful area.

Over the following weeks, her pain worsened to the point where she was hardly able to eat anything at all. She kept telling me that it was the result of weight loss, which she thought was causing her denture to become loose. Seeing that she had not appeared to have lost any weight and had previously commented about how delicious the Nacho chips were, I suspected that she was just reluctant to give up her favorite snack.

In her frustration over the pain, she asked me to contact her old dentist, who had made her upper denture, and ask for an appointment to discuss making a comparable lower denture. Not wishing to argue with my grandmother, I discussed the problem with her dentist. He said that there was little he or any dentist could do because my grandmother no longer had any lower teeth to hold the denture in place. "Even God," he said, "could not improve her lower denture without a couple of implants." The moment I heard him say that, I knew that God was going to do something miraculous.

After I told my grandmother what her dentist said, she thought about it for a while and decided that she would just have to live with the problem. I agreed that pushing for a new denture would likely not solve the problem. Not only that, but getting my grandmother back and forth to the dentist would have been a monumental task because both she and I were having difficulty walking. So I told her I would pray for her.

The day after I asked God for His help, my grandmother miraculously had a significant reduction in pain. But two days later, the pain returned with a vengeance! However, she had just finished eating the chips again. As it turned out, the brief period of improvement was just enough to convince her that the chips were the cause of the problem. So she promptly threw out the big bag of Nacho Cheese chips and promised never to eat them again. Not only that, the following day she commented that she had lost all interest in eating them!

So the double miracle was that God had given my grandmother enough relief from her pain to more clearly demonstrate the relationship between the chips and the pain, but He also removed her desire for the chips, a desire that had previously blinded her to their association with the pain.

Our Prayers are Answered

In her ninety-first year, my grandmother's vision began to deteriorate rapidly. Over a three-month period, her vision became so poor that she could no longer watch television or even dial the telephone. She even had trouble seeing the food I prepared for her. But it was not until she stopped making eye contact with me that I fully realized the magnitude of the problem.

Her doctor, a prominent ophthalmologist in the community, diagnosed her with an age-related condition for which no treatment was available. So the whole family started to pray for her. My grandmother also prayed. She said, "Oh God, not my eyes...if I have done anything wrong, please forgive me...but not my eyes, please don't take my eyes."

About half hour later, she noticed a marked improvement in her vision. The improvement progressed over the next several days to the point where her glasses were actually interfering with her vision. During the weeks that followed, she kept celebrating the fact that she could read even the fine print on the television screen. More than a year has passed, and her vision continues to be better than it had been much of her adult life!

+ + +

✝

CHAPTER 6

—⁓⁘⁓—

MIRACLES IN MY PROFESSIONAL LIFE

Physician Heal Thy Self

After about eight years in psychiatric practice, I was finding that there was a small but persistent minority patients who were not getting better. In an effort to treat the whole person, I continued to practice what I had learned as both a physician and psychotherapist by treating patients who needed medication or psychotherapy or both. I also continued to search for new ways to help suffering individuals recover their lives and their happiness. But no matter how hard I tried or where I looked for answers, there were some patients who I just could not get to a comfortable level of health.

As a resident in training nearly a decade earlier, I had discussed one of those treatment-resistant patients with a professor of psychiatry who I highly respected for his extensive training and experience. In those days, we would discuss cases using process notes; that is, detailed notes of the dialogue from each therapy session. The notes would be written immediately after each therapy session and then reviewed in a format that matched one processing session for each therapy session over a period of six months or more.

After thus reviewing a case of mine, the professor concluded that I had not been doing anything wrong. He said that I just needed to learn that there were some patients who could not be helped. When I asked him what I should tell the patient, he said, "Just tell her you cannot help her." When he said that, I thought to myself, how can I go and tell her that; it will take away her hope.

So, having exhausted all my resources, I just continued to do my best over the years without giving up on any of my treatment-resistant patients. But when further education, research, and practice did not provide the tools that would allow me to help those treatment-resistant individuals, I did the same thing I had done all my life when I had nowhere else to turn—I prayed. On my knees I said, "Lord, I don't know how to help these difficult patients, but I don't want to take away their hope. I know that you know how to help them. Please show me what to do." Contrary to what I had hoped, I received no revelations, no visions, no flashes of light—the Lord was completely silent.

Then, about three weeks later, while I was watching golf on a Sunday afternoon, I heard a soft tapping at the core of my being. What's that, I wondered? Then the Lord spoke to me: "Give Me your time," He said.

Although I knew it was the Lord God, I did not want to give Him my time. Everything was going so well in my life that I did not want to make the sacrifice. I was in good health, I had a beautiful family, I was respected by my patients and peers, and I really wanted to see who was going to win the golf tournament I was watching on television.

Then I thought to myself, the Lord has given me everything I have. So I turned to God and said, "Lord, you have given me everything I have; what would you like for me to do?" Immediately, the thought came to me: just start looking for anything on television that is about God.

So I started flashing through the channels, hoping not to find anything because I really wanted to see the end of the golf tournament. We had over fifty channels at that time, and after flipping through nearly all of them, I had not found anything spiritual. Then, with only one channel left to go, there he was, some preacher who I had never seen before. Then I thought to myself, wait, maybe the program is almost over. But when I checked the time, it was just a few minutes after the hour, and this preacher was just getting started. I thought to myself, great, there goes the golf tournament.

At first I was too unsettled to concentrate on what the minister was saying. But after about fifteen minutes, I managed to get my mind off of golf and really start paying attention to Dr. Stanley. When the sermon had ended, I again heard the knocking at the core of my being followed by the words, "give Me your time." Not knowing what to do, I said, "Lord, if I watch this program every Sunday, would that satisfy you?" And the knocking stopped.

So I made a habit of watching Charles Stanley every Sunday. After several weeks, my wife began to notice and asked me what was going on. I just told her not to worry about it. You see, it was too personal for me to share with anyone at that time.

After a while, I began to wonder whether the things I was learning from the program were really accurate. So I started to read the Bible for an hour after each sermon to verify the accuracy of Dr. Stanley's teaching.

For more than a year, I continued watching and reading every Sunday. To my surprise, I began to notice a subtle sense of peace and joy growing in my heart. Then one day, while I was sitting in my office waiting for my next patient, the Lord spoke to me again and said, "You are nothing." What! I thought. How could that be. I am a respected doctor, I am a good father, and I am well-liked by everyone. So I started to argue with God. But as I looked more deeply at myself, the Lord helped me to see that everything I was and everything I had was for my own personal gratification. I had become a physician because I wanted to be somebody; I was kind to my patients because I wanted them to like me; and I had married and had children because I wanted to have a family. As I continued to probe my mind, I was unable to find anything that was completely unselfish.

When I realized that the Lord was right, I started to feel unworthy to be a physician. I thought to myself, how can I continue to treat patients and charge them, when the Lord just finished telling me that I am nothing?

Fearing that I would have to stop practicing medicine right there and then, I started to panic. In the midst of my distress, I recalled the words I had read in the Bible during the preceding year of study. They were the words of St. Paul in his letter to the Romans: "For I know that in me dwells no good thing." Well, I thought to myself, at least I'm not alone. Then I thought, what did he do about it? And I remembered Paul's words to the Philippians: "I can do all things through Christ who strengthens me."

So I thought to myself, that's it, I have the answer. I will ask the Lord to come and live in me. So I said, "Lord, would you come and work through me? Then you can treat the patients." Immediately, I felt that He had accepted.

But instead of being satisfied with that, I started to think about all the time and effort I had invested in becoming a physician and how I would henceforth have to give God all the credit for my success with patients. As I observed myself thinking this way, I could see why the Lord said that I was nothing. Here I had the King of the Universe, the

Creator of Heaven and Earth, offering to use me as His instrument, and I was worried about who was going to get the credit. Then I was reminded that God was the One who had made me; He was the One who had given me my intelligence, my strength, my very life. So I suddenly realized that God had been behind my every accomplishment and that what I had been doing was stealing the credit from Him. That meant that all I had to do was to admit it and start giving the credit to whom it was due. Well that's easy enough, I thought.

But then there was another problem. I thought to myself, if I allow the Lord to work through me, what is He going to say or do? I am a physician and a scientist. If He starts preaching to my patients, what will they and my colleagues think? It could ruin my career!

As these thoughts were running through my mind, the Lord humbly asked, "Would you be ashamed of Me?" Disarmed by His reading of my mind and moved by His gentleness and humility, I boldly replied, "Lord, you can come and work through me even if it does ruin my career.

From that moment forward, things were not the same in my office. Oh, it was still my voice, my personality, and my mannerisms. It was still my use of reasoning and deductive skills. And to my surprise, the Lord did not start preaching to everyone. But there was one important difference, something new and wonderful that had not been there before. There was a Spirit of love that filled the room! And through that Spirit, I found myself being truly loving and compassionate to all my patients. Some of those who had known me before that day noticed the difference and asked me about it. A few commented that they just felt a strong sense of unconditional acceptance.

A short time later, a patient who I had been treating for many years asked me if there was anything she could do to express her gratitude for all the help I had given her over the years. I told her there was. I asked her to pray that God would help me to help my patients better. She said, "I will!"

The next morning, I awoke to a revolutionary new idea concerning mood disorders. The concept had taken shape in my mind like a Kodak picture that was developing before my eyes. What I was being made aware of was that the vast majority of patients who suffer from depression actually experience cycles of depression much like patients with bipolar disorder but without the highs. And because they cycle from more depressed to less depressed to more depressed again, they have a neurophysiological abnormality akin to that in patients with bipolar disorder and, therefore, ought to be treated with the same kinds of medications that are used to treat bipolar disorder.

When, with their consent, I applied this concept to my depressed patients who had not been responding to the standard treatment (mainly antidepressants), nearly all of them got better almost immediately! My success rate in treating mood disorders skyrocketed from sixty percent to greater than ninety percent, and the results got even better as I continued to perfect the technique over the next several years.

Today, there is a steadily growing body of scientific literature that supports the validity of the treatment technique I had learned to employ. The miracle is that God made me privy to the concept years before the scientific research could validate it but immediately after the necessary medications (a new line of anticonvulsants) had become available. His timing allowed hundreds of suffering patients, including most of my treatment-resistant patients, to benefit from the necessary medications long before their value in treating mood disorders had become recognized. The other part of the miracle is that during the years following my God-given breakthrough, nearly every patient who was referred to me had the specific malady that I had learned to treat. At first I thought it was coincidental, but as time went on, there were so many referrals and so many successful outcomes that it became obvious that God was selecting the patients. He had given me a hammer, and He was sending the nails. What is more, the patients He was sending me were open to the word of God and seeking to incorporate spirituality into their healing. In retrospect, the whole thing made sense; God was combining physical healing with spiritual healing, just as He had done in the person of Jesus Christ two thousand years ago.

And so, in answer to my prayer to help others, God began by healing my soul, showing me that the blind could not lead the blind. Then He helped me better understand the pathophysiology of depression so that I could heal my patients physically as well as spiritually.

Ten years later, after I had perfected what I had learned, God inspired me to put my knowledge and observations in writing for the benefit of all. The book is called Am I Depressed Or Am I Bipolar, available at www.barnesandnoble.com.

The Living Water

Recently, I met a woman in the waiting room of a doctor's office. I normally don't talk to people in waiting rooms because I tend to be quiet and contemplative, but she made a comment about the shirt I was wearing, and once we started conversing, she told me about a woman who overcame numerous health problems by switching to a specialized filtration system for her drinking water. When I asked her what it was, she said she did not remember but that she could find out and forward the information to me if I gave her my e-mail address. Well it is about as rare for me to give out my e-mail address as it is for me to talk to anyone in a waiting room. But I was interested in the water, and something beyond my reason prompted me to give her my e-mail address rather than my mailing address.

That evening she sent me an e-mail about the water. Though I decided not to pursue the filtration system, our discussion about the water ended up becoming an opportunity for me to help her medically and, more important, spiritually.

The degree to which I was inspired to minister to her, and her receptiveness to it were clear indicators that our meeting had been providential. As I continued to share the Gospel with her over the following months, the course of her medical condition made it increasingly clear that it had a divine purpose—to bring her to God.

Only in retrospect did I recognize the biblical nature of our meeting. Just as the Samaritan woman had offered Jesus water at the well, this woman had offered me water. But what God offered her through me was spiritual guidance and inspiration—the living water that Jesus offered the woman at the well.

Seek Ye First the Kingdom of God

During my first year in private practice, I had nearly two hundred thousand dollars of educational debt, a family to provide for, and very few patients.

I had only been in practice for a couple months when I admitted a patient who the attending psychiatrist no longer wanted to see because of her limited ability to pay. She was under public aid, and so any doctor who treated her was sure to take a financial loss, especially because she was a very difficult patient who required a great deal of care. I agreed to treat her nonetheless simply because I felt I had the ability to help her.

As expected, treating her was both difficult and time-consuming. Looking back on it, she required more physician time over the many years that I treated her than any other patient I have seen. The miracle in the story is that a mistake was made about her insurance. After several months of treating her, I learned that her husband had a cadillac insurance policy with no limits, a rarity at a time when HMOs and managed care were permeating the healthcare system.

I would have to estimate that nearly eighty percent of my earnings during my first two years in practice came from that one patient! And not only that, she turned out to be one of the most appreciative and successful cases I have ever had. It bore witness to the Lord's teaching: Seek ye first the kingdom of God, and his righteousness; and all these things shall be added unto you. Matthew 6:33, KJV.

Peace Through Prayer

One day I arrived at work and unexpectedly began to feel as though one of my female colleagues was really resentful of me. I could not think of any reason for it, nor had I ever before had a feeling like that about anyone in my life. Yet I continued to feel her resentment all day long. I tried to push it out of my mind or identify what had triggered it, but to no avail.

By the second day, the negativity was starting to sap my energy. So I started thinking about what to do. I thought about confronting her, but if my intuition was correct and she truly resented me, she probably would not admit it. On the other hand, if there were no real basis for my feelings, she would think I was crazy. In any case, the only sense I could make of it was that someone might have told her something negative about me, which then caused her to pass judgment. But who knows what that could have been or why. All that I knew was that the negativity was draining me.

In my desire to right the situation without confronting her, I did the only peaceable thing I could. I got on my knees before God and prayed. I simply asked God to let there be peace between her and me.

But when I came to work the following day, nothing had changed; all day I continued to feel the same irrational resentment directed at me.

So once again, I got down on my knees and prayed. But still, nothing changed. The third day, I said the same prayer.

When I returned to work the fourth day, I felt completely fine. The whole thing had apparently resolved because I again felt like there was peace between us. In the words of Dr. Charles Stanley of In Touch Ministries, I had "fought the battle on my knees"—and won. I received confirmation of this about a month later when she referred a patient to me. What made it even more convincing was that it was the first patient she had ever referred to me, and we had been colleagues for several years. It was as if the Lord were saying, this is a sign of the piece that now exists between her and you. It was yet another reminder of the awesome power of prayer.

Saved by the Golden Rule

Several years ago, I had the misfortune of covering for a colleague whose patient was complaining about the poor care she was receiving in the hospital. As I was making rounds, her nurse told me that she was demanding to be seen by a psychiatrist and threatening to file a grievance against the hospital and all the staff who were treating her. To make matters worse, I had to be out of the hospital within an hour and still had a newly admitted patient to see. The good news was that I had a Family Practice Resident working with me, but she too had to leave soon. So I sent her in to do the preliminary work on my new patient, while I attended to the disgruntled patient.

Well, just as I had picked up the patient's chart, a gynecologist who had come on to the unit asked if she could see the patient first. I told her that I was really pressed for time and kindly asked her if she could wait. But she told me she was on her way out of town and had to leave to the airport in thirty minutes.

So I thought to myself, what a mess; now one of us is going to have to make the sacrifice. By rights, the choice was mine because I had picked up the patient's chart first. Yet I could see how desperate this doctor was to get going. So I bit the bullet and handed her the patient's chart. She was very appreciative and said she would only be a short while. I reluctantly but graciously told her to take her time.

So there I was, just sitting there with nothing to do, when in fact I was pressed for time! As I sat there waiting, I questioned the wisdom of allowing that doctor to see the patient first and asked God to help me.

After about ten minutes, the gynecologist came out of the patient's room and sat down to write a note in the chart. In the meantime, the patient's nurse came up to me and said, "Dr. Binder, the patient no longer wishes to see you because the gynecologist gave her the diagnosis she was looking for. She is so happy about it that she no longer wishes to file a grievance either" So I thought to myself, not only I, but the whole treatment team was saved by the Golden Rule: do unto others as you would have them do unto you.

Obedience: the Door
to Opportunity

On one occasion, I had planned to go golfing with a friend and had taken the afternoon off. That morning the weather was absolutely beautiful, and the forecast called for sunny skies and mild temperatures throughout the day. I had a few patients to see in the morning, but at around 9:30 a.m. a small voice inside of me said, "Don't go golfing today." So I thought to myself, what! Where could this be coming from? Well it obviously wasn't coming from me, so I knew it must have been coming from above.

After a few minutes of struggling with the upsetting idea of calling off my golf plans, I reluctantly called my friend. He answered the phone full of excitement and said, "Beautiful day for golf, isn't it? I can't wait to play this afternoon!" Then, feeling even worse than I before he said that, I reluctantly told him that I did not think we should play. His response was, "What, do you have to work?" I said, "No." He said, "Then why?" And I said, "I don't know, I just have a feeling that we shouldn't play today." Sounding sad and frustrated, he said, "Well okay, we'll try again some other time." I felt so awful and upset about the whole thing that I closed the blinds in my office so that I would not be reminded of all the fun I was going to miss.

Then, at about 1130 a.m. I received a request for an emergency consult. I agreed to do it since I then knew that I was not going to be playing golf that afternoon. About a half hour later, I received another consult request. Two hours after that, one of my patients called in tears, saying that she needed to see me right away. After that, another patient called with an emergency. By one o'clock in the afternoon, my schedule was booked until eight o'clock in the evening. So I thought to myself, at least the afternoon won't be wasted.

At about three o'clock, I started to hear a soft tapping outside my office window that rapidly grew louder and louder. When I opened the blinds to see what was going on, I saw golf ball-sized hail falling from the sky! Then there was a large crack of thunder. I couldn't believe it. The forecast had been for sunny skies all day. Then I realized that the hale had started to fall at exactly the time that my friend and I had been scheduled to tee off! Suddenly I felt this great sense of joy and relief for having obeyed God. With that, I enthusiastically looked forward to serving my patients for the remainder of the day. I also thought about how badly I would have felt had I refused all those emergency requests only to be hit by golf balls instead of hitting golf balls!

No Need to Second-guess God

Many years ago, a psychotherapist that I know asked me if I would be willing to sign on as a supervisor for a psychotherapy clinic she wanted to open. I really did not want to get involved, but a small voice inside of me said, "Just do it." Having learned to be obedient to that inner voice even when it conflicts with my own logic or desire, I told her that I would.

Over the next six months, she called me on numerous occasions to discuss and have me sign various documents that were needed by the State. Eventually, the day came when she needed me to come to the office to meet with an inspector from the licensing department, a meeting that was required for her to obtain final approval and her license to practice in her new office.

However, as I was heading to work on the morning of the meeting, that same small voice that had previously told me to help her told me not to go to the meeting. I thought to myself, what! How could I do that to her? So I said, "Lord, I told you from the beginning that I did not want to get involved with this, but you told me that I should. Now, after I have fully committed myself to being her supervisor, You, at the last minute, tell me to tell her that I am not going through with it. This makes absolutely no sense."

Naturally, it made me begin to wonder whether it was really God who had told me to help her in the first place. So as I continued to drive, I said, "Lord, if you are really telling me not to go to the meeting this afternoon, I need a sign." Just as I finished saying said that, I heard the speaker on a cassette tape I had been playing in the car say, "Never cosign for a person." I thought, What? And I rewound the tape because I could not believe what I had just heard. Sure enough, that was exactly what he said. I thought to myself, God could not have given me a more convincing sign. So as soon as I got to work, I picked up the telephone and called the therapist. As I was dialing her number, I thought to myself, how am I going to explain this to her? Then I thought, well, I will just have to tell her the truth.

When she heard my voice on the telephone, she sounded excited and said, "So, I'm going to see you at 2:30 this afternoon, right?" Hesitatingly, I said, "Well..." And she said, "What's wrong? Please don't tell me that there is a problem." I said, "I can't go through with it." "Why?" she asked. "Did something happen?" I said, "No, I just suddenly got the feeling that I should not go through with it."

To my surprise, she understood. She simply said, "If you have the feeling that you should not go through with it, you should listen to that; I completely understand." She continued, "I'm sorry it didn't work out, but thank you for trying." Although I felt terrible about having had to make the phone call, I was pleasantly surprised and greatly relieved that she understood.

Late that afternoon, I received a call from her. She was full of excitement. When I asked her what happened, she said, "The inspector came, looked over everything, and asked where you were. I told him you had backed out at the last minute, to which he replied, "Well, that's okay; everything else looks good, so I'm going to approve it anyway."

The miracle in the story is that God allowed me to help this person start her clinic without allowing me to get legally involved. With my consent, God simply used me as a catalyst.

While I am glad that I was obedient to His voice, I feel badly for having questioned His judgment and His method. It taught me a powerful lesson, a lesson I will never forget: there is no need to second-guess God.

Trust the Voice Within

Several years ago, my department hired a new administrator. I remember meeting him for the first time. He was polite, friendly, and had a firm handshake. He seemed like a good addition to the department and someone who I could trust.

Despite all that, a voice within said, "Don't trust him; he's a snake." I thought to myself, what! That makes no sense. I could see nothing in his demeanor, his body language, or his tone of voice that would warrant such a negative thought. Even as a psychiatrist, I could not see anything that he said or did that would logically sound such an alarm. Anyhow, I didn't think much more about it.

The next time I ran into him, he was again very nice and even invited me into his office. We chatted for awhile about work and sports, and as I left his office, I thought about how ridiculous it was for me to think that this nice guy was "a snake."

Several months later, one of my close colleagues pulled me into her office and asked if she could speak with me. As I sat down, she broke into tears and started telling me about all the cruel things that that administrator had done to her and to several other long-standing members of the department. I had not heard such an ill report about anyone in all the years I had been working at that hospital. It immediately reminded me of what that small voice had said the first time I met him. A short time later, the department let him go.

What is so miraculous about this story is that it demonstrates that there is an intelligence outside of ourselves that is wiser than we will ever be. Call it God, call it our Higher Power, call it our guardian angel. But whatever we choose to call it, we should learn to trust it and work with it because that intelligence can do far more to help us and protect us than we could ever do for ourselves.

God Our Guide

Many years ago, I received an invitation to a national medical conference. One of the reasons I wanted to attend was that a well-known professor with a wealth of clinical experience was going to be there. Because he was so busy with patients and publishing, his time was at a premium. So I recognized this as an opportunity to have a relaxing discussion and ask him some burning questions. Ideally, I had hoped to sit at his table during the conference so that we would have plenty of time to share ideas.

Unfortunately, I arrived at the conference later than I had planned, and most of the tables were already full. Everyone was well-dressed and scholarly looking, and it seemed that most of the people who were seated already knew one another.

As I continued to stand in the doorway of the conference hall trying to decide where to sit, I asked God to direct me to the table where the professor I had hoped to meet was seated. As I was praying, my eyes caught one table where two gentlemen were sitting quietly. They appeared not to know each other, and so I thought they would be more open to receiving a stranger.

Just as I was about to head over to their table, a small voice inside of me said, "No, don't sit there"...and my gaze turned to the far corner of the room where sat one man all by himself, a man who was so homely looking that one would think he had wandered into the wrong room.

So I thought to myself, I don't want to sit there. But then I thought, that man is all alone and will probably remain all alone; to sit next to him would be the gracious thing to do. So I halfheartedly walked over to his table, politely said hello, and sat down. After a few minutes, he turned to me and introduced himself as the distinguished professor I had traveled two thousand miles to meet! Because there was no one else at our table, and the conference had not yet begun, I had the opportunity to ask him all the questions I wanted.

Just as I had finished getting my questions answered, the organizers of the conference came over and joined in with questions of their own. A few minutes later, the conference began.

During the breaks, people were lining up at our table to ask questions of this professor. Consequently, I had not only gotten my questions answered but I also got the opportunity to learn from the questions of others. As the evening wore on, I felt more and more privileged to be seated next to this professor.

God's providence in directing me to this most unlikely of persons helped me understand other amazing stories we have heard, like how God helped Joan of Arc distinguish King Charles from among the guests he pretended to be in his court, and how God helped Abraham's servant find Rebecca for his son Isaac.

Saved by the Need of Another

Several years ago, I was applying for hospital privileges and, due to extenuating circumstances, faced a critical deadline for getting in my application. The post office was ten minutes away, and I needed to put my application in the mail before they closed at 5:00 p.m.

As I was pulling out of my driveway at about twelve minutes to five, I heard the neighbor boy calling my name as he was racing toward my car. Concerned that there might be some kind of emergency, I stopped momentarily and hollered, "What is it, Michael? I have to go!" He yelled back "Wait! I have to get my dad's hammer out of your garage...he said that if I don't come home with it, I'm going to get a spanking!"

This really put me in a bind because I remembered borrowing the hammer and felt that it was my responsibility to let him get it. So I had to open the garage door for him and wait to make sure he found it. After about three or four minutes, Michael came running out of my garage with the hammer in hand, shouting thank you! thank you! thank you! I then sped off to the post office.

I arrived at exactly 5:00 p.m. As I hurried through the main door of the building, the postal clerk was pulling down the large metal cage, indicating that the office was closing. In desperation, I thought to ask her to wait a minute, but then I realized that it wouldn't be fair. Those people had been working all day, and it was time for them to go.

So I just stood there, feeling as though someone had popped my balloon and let all the air out. Realizing that there was no longer anything I could do to prevent my application from being late, I decided to take it out of the envelope and recheck everything. It was something I had not had a chance to do because I had been in such a hurry to get to the post office. As I was rechecking things, I came across a section that I had filled out improperly. It was an error that could easily have made the difference between acceptance and rejection. I corrected the error and mailed the application the following day.

Despite being a day late, the application was approved. While I may never know whether the last minute correction made the difference, I do know that the approval of the application wound up opening a big door in my life and my professional career. So the last-minute correction might have been even more critical than I thought.

The miracle in the story is that the neighbor boy slowed me down enough to recheck things on the application and make the necessary correction. I believe that when God wants to help us, He commonly does so by alerting us to the need of another, and in our effort to help them, we wind up allowing God to help us through them.

Fax From Heaven

Many years ago, God spoke to my heart, telling me to make a change in my office policy. Though the change initially challenged my faith, the new policy eventually became as comfortable as it was rewarding.

Several years later, a service that I employed in my professional practice faxed some routine documents. But instead of the documents coming to me, they went to my mother's fax machine. That was completely inexplicable because I had never told any of my business associates anything about my mother, much less her fax number. In fact, I hadn't even known that my mother had a fax machine.

Never having received anything that was for me, my mother was surprised to find my name written on the fax transmittal. In setting it aside for me, she noticed some of the content and strongly suggested that I end my association with the group that had faxed me the paperwork. In the words of my mother, "God made these papers come to me because He wanted me to tell you to stop what you are doing."

Because her counsel was contrary to what I thought God, years earlier, had told me to do, I would not have obeyed my mother had it not been for the inexplicable fax transmittal. I also realized that for me not to listen to my mother would itself have been contrary to God, especially after He had shown me personally what a high value He placed on obedience to my mother. So I just did what my mother told me to do.

As of the writing of this book, three years have passed, and I can now clearly see that God had been speaking through my mother after He had gotten my attention by rerouting the fax. The changes I made in my office practice in accordance with my mother's advice turned out to be absolutely critical, possibly even life-saving!

Some people might argue that the misdirected fax was merely a coincidence, for even if God had been trying to communicate an idea, why, they might ask, would He have done it in such a strange way? I think the answer lies in the fact that He was trying to communicate a directive that was contrary to what He had previously instructed me to do. What's more, His original directive was something that the Bible tells us we aught to do. So if God were to have communicated with me in the same way that He had His original directive, I most likely would have ignored it. I even ignored it when He tried to communicate it through my mother a few weeks before she received the misdirected fax. So what God did was to combine the change in His counsel with an inexplicable occurrence in an effort to get my attention.

Through experience, I have found that God communicates with us in at least six fundamental ways: Through His word, through divine inspiration, through the counsel of others, through the circumstances of our life, through dreams, and sometimes through odd coincidences or unusual occurrences, such as this. That's why we need to be mindful of God at all times. The more in tune we are with Him, the more likely we will be to hear Him and, thus, receive His blessings.

+ + +

✝

CHAPTER 7

—❧✝❧—

MIRACLES IN MY PERSONAL LIFE

"Don't Eat Sugar"

One evening when I was about thirty-five years old, I suddenly and unexpectedly heard a voice inside say, "Don't eat sugar." Although I assumed that it was the Lord whispering to me about my health, I thought it strange that He would tell me to avoid sugar when all the research held that cholesterol was the main instigator of bad health. But having learned to obey the Lord unquestioningly, I decided that I would henceforth try to avoid all sweets.

Well, that very night I met my first test. After finishing dinner, I had a mind to eat some delicious chocolate chip cookies my wife had bought for the kids. As I opened the cupboard, I remembered what the voice had told me, and so I tried to stop myself. However, the urge was too strong; I just had to have at least one of those cookies. So as I reached into the package, I said, "Lord, if it was really you telling me not to eat sugar, I am really gonna need your help because I can't resist eating one of these cookies!" With that said, I took a bite of a cookie.

Surprisingly, it did not taste as good as I thought it would. Moments later, I developed a kind of sick feeling. It was then that I knew for certain that it had been the voice of the Lord telling me not to eat sugar anymore. So I renewed my commitment to avoid all sweets, and avoid them I did. I completely stopped eating cake, cookies, and frosted cereal. I stopped putting sugar in my oatmeal, and I even stopped my favorite dinner drink—Mott's apple juice.

A few months later, I heard a lecture by a highly respected professor of medicine and nutrition. To my surprise, her focus was on sugar rather than cholesterol as the main detriment to our health. She had been discussing new research that suggested that refined sugar was actually far more dangerous to our health than cholesterol. It immediately reminded me of the Lord's counsel about sugar. In the years to follow, I would learn the mechanisms by which refined sugar could lead not only to diabetes and atherosclerosis but to a host of other chronic health conditions because of its unhealthy effects on metabolism.

A Lesson in Money Management

The roots of this story go back to my childhood. When I was about ten years old, I was playing a card game called "war" with my best friend Steve. We were playing for pennies, and about an hour into the game, I had lost all but my last penny. Out of desperation, I said, "Please Lord, let me win back my money. In return, I promise that I will never gamble again."

From that point onward, I began to win one card draw after another until I had won back all my money. Then I abruptly quit. Naturally, Steve became very upset and said that we had to keep playing. But I refused, having been satisfied with the miracle of winning back my money. Afterward, I again thanked God for answering my prayer and repeated my promise never to gamble again.

I faithfully kept that promise until thirty years later, when I decided to invest in some stocks. I suppose that at the time, I did not quite see it as gambling, but the Lord apparently did, as we shall see.

In my first investment, I gained about three thousand dollars over a six-month period. Then the market tanked, and in just one week I lost more than I had gained. I was so upset about it that I again found myself asking God to bail me out.

God's response was that I should immediately withdraw my money from the stock market. But wait a minute, I thought, I'm down nearly a thousand dollars, and if I pull out now, I will take a loss. But the Lord had spoken, and I knew the ball was in my court.

So I found myself having to chose between my logic and my faith. Having asked God for help, I decided to obey Him. That afternoon, I withdrew all my money from the market and accepted my loss.

When I checked the closing value of my stock the next morning, I was shocked to find that I had broken even. The market had unexpectedly jumped sharply at the end of the day, and I had regained all the money I had lost!

Unfortunately, I still had not learned my lesson. Several years later, I was again investing, this time in retirement accounts. Once again, I did not quite view it as gambling; I was simply preparing for my retirement. Yet a part of me recognized the inconsistency in believing that I could trust God to give me a long life but not trust Him to give me my daily bread, especially if I were to use my extra money to help those in need. Still, I rationalized what I was doing by telling myself that my extra money would be worth more for charity at the age of retirement than at the time of my investment because of the tax break I would receive.

Then one day, after years of watching my retirement accounts grow, I received a call from my son, asking me whether it was wise to invest in the stock market. I warned him not to and explained it like this: if you lose, you will wish you had never played; and if you win, you will find yourself relying more on your money than on God. So either way, it would be a bad idea. He said he understood and thanked me.

The problem is that I did not take my own advice, reasoning that my retirement accounts were different. Six months later I, like so many others, suffered the effects of the market crash in the Fall of 2008. Once again, I found myself asking God to let me break even. Between that and my mother's urging, I pulled out early enough to come out ahead. But several months later, I received a letter explaining that one of my account holders had been sending my mail to an old address. By the time the mail caught up with me, I had incurred a big loss on that investment and had just enough money left in the account to break even overall. Though I was disappointed, I realized that my prayer had been answered—I had asked God to let me break even—and He did.

In gratitude to God and obedience to my mother, I accepted the loss on that old account and pulled all the money out even though I felt confident that the market would eventually rebound with the help of the stimulus package.

Today, I no longer invest in stocks. I have discovered a far better way to handle excess money: invest in God by simply donating it to charity. It's the kind of investment that benefits everyone, and most of all, one's self by keeping one's eyes focused on God, who is our true benefactor.

St. Joan, St. Catherine & Dr. McCann

About ten years ago, I was visiting my uncle in San Francisco, and we stopped at a video store to rent a movie for the evening. He told me to pick anything I wanted, so I asked the attendant if they had Braveheart, a movie I had seen in the theatre and wanted my uncle to see. The attendant told me that they had the movie but that it was a new release and really wasn't to be rented out for another three days. Nonetheless, he offered to rent it to us. Though the attendant was willing to bend the rules for me, and though I really wanted to see that movie, I expressed my concern that the attendant would be putting himself at risk. So I bit the bullet and went looking for another movie. Suddenly, I thought of Joan of Arc. The idea was so powerful and unexpected that I felt as though it had come from above. Not surprisingly, the movie was readily available.

Though I thought I had seen the movie before, I was surprised to find that I had not seen it in its entirety. I had actually only seen the first half of the film. In its entirety, the movie turned out to be so moving that I watched it four times that weekend. I felt that the viewing had been arranged by God, who wanted to reward me for caring about the attendant at the video store and saw that I had plenty of time available to watch this powerfully inspirational film.

Sometime after that, I was at a bookstore looking for books that were written by Saints. After about three hours of searching, I had looked through every book in the spirituality section, or so I thought, and was leaving the store when a soft voice told me to go back to the book shelf because I had missed something. As I turned around and walked back to the same bookshelf that I had just finished looking through, I asked myself what I could have missed. Just then, my eyes fell on one book that was sticking out slightly. I took the book down, opened it somewhere in the center, and after reading one paragraph, I thought to myself, this is the greatest book I have ever read! I then bought two copies without any further ado.

It was not until late that evening that I had a chance to pick the book up again. At the end of the twenty-five page introduction, I discovered that the book was written by St. Catherine of Siena, who at that time was one of only two women doctors of the Catholic Church. The book is called *The Dialogue* because in it, St. Catherine asks God questions, and He gives her answers in visions that she dictated to her confessors in the fourteenth century.

As I was reading the book, I began to see the connection between Catherine of Siena and Joan of Arc, these two saints God had guided me to. I learned that St. Catherine was the one to whom Joan of Arc referred at her trial as having been chosen by God to guide her on her mission to save France.

In an effort to investigate this further, I purchased a comprehensive book of Saints of the Catholic Church. In it I discovered striking similarities between the lives of St. Catherine and St. Joan. Both cut their hair short and never married in an effort to dedicate their lives to God. Also, both were politically active in Europe during the medieval period. St. Catherine tried and succeeded in brokering peace between the English and the Florentines in Italy, and St. Joan succeeded in ending the One-hundred-years-war between England and France. And like St. Catherine, St. Joan was betrayed by her countrymen and had been robbed of the satisfaction of seeing her work to its ultimate completion. Thus, it is not surprising that God had chosen Catherine to help Joan in her efforts to save France. What is so miraculous and spiritually enlightening about this is that Catherine's work in guiding Joan from above demonstrates how we can continue in the hereafter the work we had begun on earth.

A very recent example of this occurred during the summer of 2005, when Dr. Michael McCann, a dear friend and mentor of mine, passed away. His chief concern had always been his handicapped son Gregory. He worried about who would care for Greg after he died. As fate would have it, Greg got lost the day after Dr. McCann died. He had been waiting for a family friend to pick him up at a bus stop, and the friend forgot to get him until two hours later. By then Greg was gone. That created a major problem because Greg loved to ride buses and could have been anywhere in Los Angeles.

In the meantime, another family friend, who was not aware that Greg was missing, was driving somewhere in Los Angeles when she suddenly heard the voice of Michael McCann say, "Look to your right." She initially ignored it and thought to herself, why is Michael McCann talking to me? Then she again heard the voice say, "Look to your right." This time she could not resist. When she looked to her right, there Greg was walking down the street by himself. She pulled over and asked Craig where he was going. He said, "I'm lost, I'm lost..." So she drove him home.

So if ever we wonder what we do when we leave this world, the answer appears to be very simple: the same thing we began in this world.

The Chapel of St. Joan of Arc

For as long as I can remember, I have been intrigued and inspired by the life of St. Joan of Arc. The interesting thing about it is that I had those feelings long before I knew anything about her life or place in history. As a college student, I would read about the lives of the Saints, but I had never read anything about the life of Joan of Arc. Then one day, as I explained in the previous memoir, I was inspired to rent the movie Joan of Arc, played by actress Leelee Sobieski. I was so moved by her story that I subsequently researched and watched other films about her life, including the 1961 adaptation with actress Ingrid Bergman and the 1929 silent film directed by Carl Dreyer. I also read about her life in novels by John Beavers and Mark Twain. To say that her story drew me to her would not be quite right. I believe that I became drawn to her story because I already knew her in spirit.

Be that as it may, I one day learned from one of my patients in Wisconsin that the little chapel in which St. Joan regularly prayed in her village in Domrémy France had been moved brick by brick to the nearby campus of Marquette University.

I immediately decided to visit the chapel, but several weeks passed before I found a chance to do so. Finally, one Sunday morning at about 9:30 a.m., I found the opportunity to go. But a small voice inside of me said, "Wait, don't go yet." So I cleaned my apartment for about an hour and a half, after which I felt free to be on my way.

When I arrived at the campus of Marquette University, I initially had trouble finding the chapel. Then suddenly there it was, a small stone structure with stained glass windows and heavy wooden doors with large that made you feel as though you were back in the medieval days. The foundation area was made of white cobblestone, and the chapel itself was surrounded by trees budding delicate white flowers. As I approached the sacred shrine, the same small voice again told me to wait.

So I sat down on a nearby bench and began to pray. After about ten minutes, I felt free to continue on toward the chapel. As I drew near to it, there was no one around except for some college students standing near the front entrance chatting. Then a middle-aged woman, who appeared to be the custodian, walked along side the chapel, reverently kissed one of the blossoms on an overhanging tree, and disappeared into a side door.

So I thought to myself, I ought to show the same kind of reverence for this holy place as that woman did when she kissed that blossom. But kissing a flower seemed like too effeminate a thing for me to do, especially in the presence of the students who were standing there.

As I was thinking about it, I sensed Joan say to me, "I denied my femininity for God; can you deny your masculinity for Him?" So I humbled myself and kissed one of the flowers regardless of what the students might have thought. Just as I did that, my sense of embarrassment gave way to a spirit of welcome that drew me to the front entrance of the chapel. As I was about to pull open the large wooden door, I noticed an engraving in the wall that read, "The tomb of a hero is in the hearts of the living." Then I noticed a little sign stuck in the ground that read, "Visitation hours: Sundays noon to 4:00 p.m. only." As I was reading the sign, the noon bells from a near-by church began to sound. That was the first miracle. I then pulled open the door and entered the austere, musty memorial to the holy life of St. Joan of Arc.

After looking around for a moment, I knelt down in prayer. How long I remained in meditation I do not know, but I could clearly sense Joan's welcoming presence amidst the calm, cool, quiet of that austere little place. There were a few placards on the wall and a small armor statue of the saint, but aside from that, the chapel was barren. As I was looking at the miniature statue, I began to wonder what Joan really looked like and how tall she really was. Just then, the custodian walked out from the sacristy to greet me, so I took the liberty to ask her if she knew what Joan really looked like. To my amazement, she said that the statue was true to life in both size and appearance. I told her that I could hardly believe it because it was so tiny. The custodian smiled and said that Joan was only four feet, nine inches tall. After that, I sat down for awhile to ponder the enigmatic wisdom of God in choosing this tiny illiterate girl from a peasant farm to lead the entire French army. I thought to myself, truly God uses the humble and the meek over the prideful and the strong.

As I was preparing to exit the chapel, I noticed a sign-in ledger and a book summarizing the lectures and events of Joan of Arc Week, which had recently been held on campus. The last page of the book read, "What do I have to do to be a saint?" It said, "Obey God, pray often, be kind to others, and don't be afraid to let people see that you're a little crazy."

As I stood up to leave after what seemed like about fifteen or twenty minutes, I noticed that I had actually been there nearly four hours! What's more, I felt as though I had spent the afternoon with Joan herself. I really mean it. I felt like we had been walking through a park together or sipping tea at a café. That was the second miracle.

That warm feeling remained with me for the remainder of the day. It affirmed for me just how spiritual relationships really are and that the dead, though departed, can still be with us even if we had never met them in life. That was the third miracle.

Meeting at the Well

At the age of thirty-three, I awoke one morning with the most wonderful feeling I had ever had. I awoke with the sense that God's will for my life was crystal clear to me. As I began to look around the room, the feeling of certainty began to fade rapidly until I felt back to my normal self. As I scrambled to understand where that wonderful feeling had come from, I realized that I had awoken from a dream. Over the days that followed, I gradually put the pieces of the dream together.

In the dream, I had been walking down a sun-baked dessert road somewhere in the middle east. It was Sunday morning, and I was walking an uphill path toward a church at the top of the hill where there was going to be a sermon. The hot sun was beating down on my head, and I was both thirsty and hungry, for I had not eaten breakfast in anticipation of receiving Holy Communion at the mass.

As I continued to make my way up the road, I noticed that there were sacks of bread atop the ledges of the stone walls that led to the church. As I contemplated eating some of the bread, I saw a water fountain further ahead on the side of the road. On the opposite side of the road was a poor homeless man sitting on a large stone. He was unkept and unshaven, and I suspected that he would use my visit to the well as an opportunity to ask me for some money. Preferring to avoid an uncomfortable interaction, I considered skipping the well despite my thirst. But then I thought better of it and decided to stop for a drink anyway. I did not feel it would be right to avoid the well just to avoid a needy stranger.

Then sure enough, just as I bent over to have a drink, the homeless man was upon me. So before taking a sip, I stopped and looked up at him, assuming that he would ask me for something. But to my surprise, he looked into my eyes as if he had something to give me, something that would satisfy my hunger and thirst. As I thought about that, I began to notice something like bubbles forming on my face. So I placed my hands on my face to see what it was. When I removed my hands from my face, they removed a mask made of something like bread. Surprisingly, it was not a mask of my face but of his face, and without speaking, he made me understand that that was what I should eat. Then I remembered that it was in the moment I had swallowed a piece of the bread that the wonderful feeling I had awoken in bed with had come over me.

In retrospect, I realized that the homeless man was the Lord Jesus Christ. Seeing that I was thirsty, He met me at the well to give me water to drink—living water, just as He had given to the Samaritan woman in the Biblical story. And seeing that I was hungry, He gave me bread to eat—His body, signified by the bread that formed on my face in the image of His face and giving me the mind of God to know His will for my life.

But more than a blessing and a prophetic dream, the experience taught me not to make assumptions about people based on their appearance. Had I ignored the homeless man, I would have ignored the Lord Himself, who we know from the Bible was in fact poor and homeless. What is more, the Lord said, "Inasmuch as ye have done it unto one of the least of these my brethren, ye have done it unto me." Matthew 25:40, KJV

A Prophetic Dream

On another occasion, I dreamt that the Lord was crucified every year at Easter, and this time I was present at the crucifixion. As I stood in the crowd looking at Jesus with His head down, all bloodied and crowned with thorns, I thought to myself, is it fair that the same man should have to go through this every year?

As Pontius Pilate was washing his hands of the matter, the idea of taking Jesus' place suddenly crossed my mind. As I imagined myself pushing through the crowd and telling the Roman authorities that I wanted to take His place, I experienced the most dreadful feeling of terror I have ever known.

As I was trying to decide whether or not to do it, I was saved by the thought that I could not take His place because I am a sinner, and this sacrifice could be made only by one who was without sin. Oh what a relief I felt! So I followed the procession to a place where they began to nail Jesus to the cross. Seeing that some risers had been built around the place where the cross had been secured into the ground, I rushed to the top level, which placed me immediately behind Jesus's head. As I looked on, He turned His head all the way around, looked at me, and without actually speaking said, "You will take my place—by obeying everything I ask you to do."

Come Follow Me, Saith the Lord

I had just finished watching an old Billy Graham sermon and was moved to renew my commitment to Jesus Christ. For many years now, I have been committed to serving God, but after that sermon, I made the decision to follow Christ wholeheartedly.

As I was driving to church the following day, I saw what appeared to be the figure of Jesus affixed to a cross on the back of a work truck in front of me. Though it was nearly life-sized, I was trailing too far behind to make out the detail.

After a few miles of following it, I remembered the commitment I had made the previous night, that I would follow Jesus wholeheartedly. Suddenly, I realized that He was telling me something; He was telling me that He had accepted my commitment. As I continued to follow him, I was moved to the point of tears.

Without deviating from my natural route to church, I continued to follow him for several miles. Then I began to wonder: was this really a sign from God, or was it just a coincidence? So I said to myself, if this truck exits at Touhy Avenue East, which was where I needed to exit to get to church, then I will know it is from God.

So I continued to follow the truck and the Lord for a few more miles. When the truck reached Touhy Avenue East, it sure enough signaled to exit and I right behind it! It then continued in front of me on Touhy Avenue until I had become completely convinced that it was from the Lord. Then it turned off my path.

Tears of Joy

There was a time in my life when I was so filled with happiness that I broke into tears. I had been outside jogging at the time, and as I continued to run, I kept thanking God for all the joy he had given me. Just then, I began to feel raindrops hitting my face and mixing with my tears. I immediately saw it as God sharing my joy; I felt like He was literally crying with me!

But then the logical side of me began to wonder, were these really tears from heaven, or was this just the coincidental start of an afternoon shower? So I asked God for a sign.

Just when I stopped crying, the rain also stopped, and a rainbow appeared!

God Helps Those Who Help Themselves

Recently, my combination lock mysteriously disappeared as I was getting dressed in the locker room at the local gym. I had just opened my locker and had stepped away for a moment only to find that my lock was nowhere to be found when I went to lock up. It was really strange, especially because there was scarcely anyone else in the locker room. For the next fifteen minutes, I kept looking for the lock but found nothing. So I left in complete frustration, not only because of the ridiculousness of what had happened but also because I had to leave the gym with my locker unlocked and was growing late for an appointment.

The incident remained on my mind for the rest of the day, not so much because I had lost an ordinary lock but because the whole thing was so inexplicable. In addition, that particular lock was one of those keepers that had an easy-to-remember combination and was very forgiving when lining up the numbers. Anyhow, I really wanted it back.

As I was going to bed that night, I asked God why this strange thing had happened. I also asked Him to help me get my lock back. His response was, "Don't worry; you'll get your lock back."

The next day, I stopped at the gym's lost-and-found. When I explained what had happened, the attendant went to the back room and returned with a box full of locks, most of which looked just like mine. With a look of surprise, I asked, "All these?" She said, "Yes, people turn them in all the time." "I don't get it," I said. "Why in the world are so many people losing their locks? And why aren't they claiming them?"

She said she had no idea. So I checked all the locks against my combination, but none of them opened.

When I returned to the gym the following day, I again looked for my lock but did not find it either around my locker or in the lost-and-found. However, the attendant told me that someone had called and said he had found a lock a few days earlier but had forgotten to turn it in. Of course, I felt certain it was mine, and so I asked the attendant to call me as soon as the person returned it.

Two days later, she had the lock waiting for me at the front desk. It was in a plastic bag with my name on it! Surprisingly, however, it did not match my combination. Just one more lock for the collection basket, I thought.

The following day, I asked a person in the locker room if he had seen my lock. He told me that he had indeed found a lock. But once again, it did not turn out to be mine. However, the fact that he was holding on to it without turning it in made me wonder whether someone had found my lock and was likewise not turning it in. So I thought perhaps I should tape a note above my locker asking anyone who might have found my lock to turn it in to the lost-and-found.

As I was thinking about writing the note, I asked two guys who I saw standing together in the locker room whether they had found my lock. One of them suggested that I check the lost-and-found. The other started laughing and exclaimed, "You mean someone stole your lock!" I said, "I don't think so. I just think maybe someone found it and for whatever reason did not turn it in." But he continued to laugh saying, "I can't believe someone would steal a lock they can't even use." His comment just reminded me of how ridiculous the whole thing was, and I proceeded to the pool for my swim.

As I was walking toward my locker after returning from the pool, I again saw the guy who had been laughing about what happened. When he saw me, he called me into the television room and, pointing to a combination lock on the table, asked, "Is that your lock?" I told him it looked like it mine. When he saw me open it, he told me he had found it on top of the lockers a few days earlier and had taken it because he had assumed someone had forgotten it, and he was afraid that the cleaning people might throw it away. Relieved to have my lock back, I graciously thanked him and left it at that.

That evening, I thanked God for helping me get my lock back. I also thanked Him for two important lessons I had learned from the experience. The first is that God stands ready to help us regardless of how trivial our request. The other is that we must do our part if we wish to see our prayers answered. In this instance, God had done His part by allowing me to run into the very person who had found my lock, and I had done my part by trusting in God rather than giving up or becoming accusatory. Had I given up, I would not have inquired about the lock; and had I become accusatory and agreed with the guy who had been laughingly accusing someone of stealing my lock, I unknowingly would have been accusing the very person who had found the lock, and I doubt that he would have returned it to me. It reminded me of something St. Joan of Arc told the French army when the invading English outnumbered them four-to-one. She told them: "It is not enough that God is on our side...we also must be on His side." And with that, she forbade the soldiers to gamble in the camp, use foul language, or associate with camp-following strumpets. Of course, my situation cannot be compared to St. Joan's in terms of gravity, but in principle it is the same. When we ask God for help, we must remind ourselves of what the word "help" really means. It means two or more persons working toward a common goal. So often, we ask God for help while we ourselves are working at odds with Him, such as when we ask Him to heal an emotional wound while we continue to hold resentment toward those who have hurt us, or when a nation prays for peace while launching preemptive military strikes against another nation. We must remember that God is a team-player who, more than anything else, desires a relationship with us. Accordingly, He works with us to accomplish our goals, allowing us to do for ourselves that which we can, and doing for us that which we cannot. Put another way, God helps those who help themselves.

You Can Rely on God

I was born with a large mole on the side of my leg that I was becoming concerned about as I got older. When I was in my thirties, a relative referred me to a plastic surgeon, who looked at the mole and discussed my options. After some debate, I decided to have it removed.

But after I had returned home from the procedure, I took notice of a smaller mole on my abdomen. I had felt so relieved about having had the larger mole removed that I considered going back to the surgeon to have the smaller one removed as well. The problem was that my insurance was going to terminate before I could get back in to see him. So I started to wonder whether it was really worth having the smaller one removed anyway.

Feeling unsure about what to do, I asked God for help. I said, "Lord, you alone know whether or not this mole will ever become cancerous. If it is destined to change, let me know to have it removed; but if not, I neither want to waste the doctor's time or my money." With that in mind, I tried to be strong in my faith and leave it in God's hands. After a few days of struggle, I managed to let go of my worry and leave it to God.

Several years passed, and I had long since forgotten about the mole when I began to notice a small red growth increasing in size on my neck. After several months, I started to think that I should see my dermatologist about it.

I eventually scheduled an appointment, but when I walked into the doctor's office, the first thing he wanted to know was whether I had a family history of skin cancer. I was a little surprised by the question because I had seen him once before and already had a treatment record. In any case, I told him my father had malignant melanoma. When he heard that, he immediately asked me to remove all my clothes so that he could examine my entire body. After looking me over, he told me that everything looked okay except for one mole. It was the mole on my abdomen that I had entrusted to God but had long since forgotten about. He told me that it probably should be removed because it was larger than the size of an eraser head. He offered to do it right there and then.

The next thing I knew, I was laying on my back with sterile drapes on my abdomen, having the mole removed. After the doctor had applied the bandages, I got dressed, and just as I was getting ready to leave the office, he said, almost as an afterthought, "Oh yea, what was it you came to see me about? Did you say there was something on your neck?"

I thought to myself, oh my gosh, I almost forgot to show him the thing I came here for! So the doctor took a look at the growth on my neck and said, rather casually, "I'm not sure what that is, but this'll take care of it." And he burned it off with a few zaps from an electrocautery knife.

As I was leaving the office, I thought to myself, can you believe it? I came to see the doctor about this thing on my neck, having long forgotten about the mole on my abdomen, and the mole on my abdomen wound up being the central focus of the appointment. That's what happens when you entrust something to God!

What God Sees in Secret, He Rewards Openly

It was the first heavy snow of the winter, and I woke up that morning to find my driveway covered with three feet of snow! For some reason, I could not find a shovel in the garage, and I only had about fifteen minutes to clear a path for my car to get down the driveway for work.

Seeing that my neighbor's driveway had been cleared and that his garage door was open, I walked over and asked his wife Marjean if I could borrow a shovel. She graciously loaned me one, and I began to shovel my driveway as quickly as possible. The snow was so deep that I could barely make any headway. Marjean then came over with a snowblower. I quickly found that it was too small for the job, and so I told her that I thought I could make more headway with the shovel.

Just as I managed to clear a small area of the driveway, a big plow truck from the city came through the subdivision and pushed all the snow from the street back onto my driveway, burying me up to my chest. I tried to stop him, but he couldn't hear me because he was seated high up in this loud truck and was wearing headphones.

So there I was, covered in snow and running out of time to get to work. Not only that, but my poor neighbor, who had gotten up early in the morning and had thoroughly shoveled his driveway before heading off to work, would have to shovel again because that plow truck had pushed the snow back into his driveway too.

So I thought to myself, if it weren't for my neighbor lending me his shovel, I would not be able to shovel at all. So I decided that the gracious thing to do would be to walk over and shovel out his driveway in gratitude for having loaned me the shovel. Of course, my next thought was, but who is gonna shovel my driveway? I had patients scheduled until ten o'clock in the evening, and I feared that if temperatures dropped below zero, I was going to have a major problem because the snow would freeze, and there was no place in the cul-de-sac to park my car.

Well as crazy as this might sound, I trudged over to my neighbor's driveway and began to shovel it out for him. But just as I was about to get started, I thought to myself: you know, I am about to make this big sacrifice and go through all this work, and my neighbor won't even know it because he did not see that plow truck come through here nor is his wife likely to see me shoveling their driveway. Thus, I realized that I was not going to receive any credit for the enormous sacrifice I was about to make. So I thought to myself, what am I going to do? shall I knock on the door and say, Hey Marjean, come and see what I am about to do for you and Don? Thus, I realized that if I shoved their driveway, the only one who was going to see me was my Father in heaven. Well, I thought, that will be enough for me. So I started shoveling these big, heavy chunks of ice and snow off my neighbor's driveway. I quickly realized that the debris left by that plow truck was far more difficult to deal with than the soft white snow. I can remember some of those ice chunks being so heavy that I almost busted my back!Anyhow, I finished shoveling out my neighbor's driveway with just enough time to shower and get to work.

Because my driveway was still completely unshoveled, I had to race my car out of the garage and allow it to slide down the driveway onto the cul-de-sac. But the big question was, how was I going to get it back up the driveway when I returned home from work?

Just as I had feared, the temperature plummeted that night. As I approached my dark, cold driveway after work, I could hear the wind howling and could not, for the life of me, figure out what I was going to do. Then I noticed that my entire driveway had been plowed! Not only that, it was perfectly manicured!!! With a sigh of relief, I drove right up into my garage and went straight to bed.

The next morning, I started to investigate who had shoveled my driveway. Assuming that it was my neighbor, I called Don to thank him. But he didn't know what I was talking about. So I asked his wife if she had seen anyone come by and plow my driveway. To my astonishment, she said she had done it! I could not believe it, not only because it was such a big job but also because she had just had a baby and was still nursing.

The miracle of the story is that my neighbor could not have seen me shoveling her driveway because if she had, she would not have allowed it, knowing that I had my own driveway to shovel. Moreover, I don't see how Marjean could have done it even if she had wanted to because she had just given birth to her second child and was still at home nursing. Besides that, the tiny snowblower she had was no match for my large driveway. The other amazing thing is that Don and Marjean had never volunteered to help me with anything either before or after that day, and we had been neighbors for five years. All that left only one explanation: "What God sees in secret, He rewards openly."

God is Watching

Ever since I was in grade school, I have enjoyed hitting golf balls in the park. While I was out hitting balls one day, I found several baseballs in the outfield grass. I assumed they had been left over from a little league game or practice. Some of the balls were relatively new, so I considered keeping them for my son. But then I thought better of it and decided to leave them there for whoever had lost them. Better yet, I gathered them together and set them neatly on home plate. Then I finished hitting my golf balls, retrieved as many as I could find, and left.

When I returned to the park a week later, there were a bunch of golf balls neatly placed in the hitting area I normally use. From what I could tell, most of them were mine, and the total number was about the same as the number of baseballs I had left on home plate the previous week. It was as if somebody had been watching me gather up the baseballs and wanted to return the favor. I know that I had been the only one in the park that day, so the thing was really quite magical. It reminded me of the day I had shoveled out my neighbor's driveway after that city plow truck had come through. If there is any doubt that these things are more than coincidental, consider this next story.

While showering at the local gym, I saw a beautiful pair of swim goggles hanging outside the shower stall. They were the most beautiful goggles I had ever seen. I was the only one in the locker room, so I assumed that someone (an olympic swimmer perhaps) had simply forgotten them there. Given that I have always had difficulty finding swim goggles that I like, I was really tempted to keep them. But then I decided to do the right thing and turn them in to the Lost And Found.

Afterward, I just couldn't get those goggles out of my mind. A few days later, I came up with an idea. I thought I would wait about three weeks and then check with the lifeguard to see if anyone had claimed them. I thought perhaps the guard would give them to me if no one had claimed them by then.

So I patiently waited a few weeks, after which I asked the lifeguard if anyone had claimed the goggles. He pulled out a box of goggles, most of which were broken or cheap children's goggles, but the nice ones weren't there. That was no surprise to me. I didn't expect anyone to let *those* goggles sit in that box for very long.

About two weeks later, I had gone to Walmart for my grandmother, and as I was leaving the store, I happened to notice a stack of swim goggles hanging on the shelf. When I looked at them closely, I noticed that the pair on the top were almost identical to the goggles I had seen in the shower room. I couldn't believe it! At Walmart, I thought? And they were only thirteen dollars. Interestingly, there was only one pair of them. All the others were cheap-looking goggles—ones I did not like. That one pair also turned out to fit better than any goggles I had ever worn.

About a month later, I was at Walmart again and looked to see if they had any more of those beautiful goggles in stock. They didn't. In fact, I never saw them at Walmart again. I couldn't even find them at an exclusive swim shop I go to!

He Shut the Eyes of the Buyers

When I put my house in Wisconsin up for sale several years ago, God was again there to help me, t his time without my even asking. I had hired with a realtor, and I had reason to believe that she was working hard to sell the property because there were potential buyers walking through my house nearly every day. Yet after six months on the market, we had not had a single offer. This was really surprising because it was a standard home, and my next door neighbor, who had a similar home in the same price range, had recently sold his property after only three months.

But even after another six months and over a hundred more perspective buyers, I had still not had a single offer! Then one day I came home from work and noticed that a large picture of Jesus that I had on the mantle was missing. At first I thought perhaps one of the perspective buyers had walked off with it. But later, I found it on the floor faced down so that no one could see it. I could only assume that the realtor had taken it down under the sad assumption that it was putting off perspective buyers. So I thought to myself, maybe it is, but I'm putting it back where it belongs anyway.

After another six months without an offer, my mother convinced me to get a new realtor. So I hired someone who was very familiar with the style home I was trying to sell and who recognized the reputation of the builder. Don Ayer had been selling Trustway homes for many years and was really excited about selling my property, especially because he thought it was such a beautiful home.

But even after three months with Don, still not a single offer. So I suggested that we lower the price. "No, that's not the problem," Don said. "I've been selling homes in this area for twenty-five years, and I've never seen anything like this." He just sat there scratching his head, saying that he could not understand what was going on.

Meanwhile, I had been noticing for quite some time that my checking account was slowly growing rather than just balancing out the way it had done in previous months.

Then finally, after yet another six months on the market with the new realtor, my first offer. Though it was ten percent lower than our asking price, Don suggested that I accept it, and I did. But when I notified the bank about the offer, I was told that the total of what I still owed on the house, including my triple mortgage, was forty thousand dollars more than the bid I had received. So I was told that I would have to come up with forty thousand dollars in order for the bank to release the lean so that I could sell the house.

I really never thought about that, but by then the amount I had accrued in my checking account was forty thousand dollars plus some change—just enough to pay off the bank! Afterward, I thought about what would have happened had there been an earlier bid. The bank would have told me that I would either have to come up with forty thousand dollars (which I would not have had at that time nor would I have been able to borrow because the house had already been triple mortgaged), or I would have to raise the asking price on the house. Either way, I would not have been able to sell the house. Worse yet, I probably would have had to take it off the market, which would have left me in a catch twenty-two.

The miracle is that God had put off all prospective buyers until I had accrued enough cash to sell the house! So perhaps my first realtor was right; maybe that picture of Jesus on the mantle did have something to do with it—but not in the way she thought. Little did she know that He was actually my knight in shining armor who was holding down the fort until the time was right. It is also interesting to note that the couple who bought the house had fallen head over heals in love with it and told my realtor that they would have no other. So perhaps it was also for their sake that God had shut the eyes of the buyers.

God's Perfect Timing

As I was writing a progress note in my Waukesha office late one afternoon, I was interrupted by the thought that I should make a telephone call before the end of the day. I had been inquiring about some office space in Highland Park because I felt that it was time to move my practice to my hometown. It was close to 5:00 p.m. on Friday, so I glanced at my watch to see if I still had time to make a call. Well it was exactly 4:59 p.m. So I picked up the phone and quickly dialed, hoping to catch the secretary at Highland Park Hospital (where I had been applying for privileges) before she went home for the weekend. She answered and said she was just heading out but was glad that I called because some office space had just opened up about an hour earlier, and there was already another perspective buyer. That was not surprising because office space in the professional building of Highland Park Hospital was at a premium and rarely became available. She gave me the telephone number of the seller, who I called immediately. She agreed to meet with me the following morning.

My mother offered to come along on short notice, and we met with the seller early Saturday morning. Although the office was a golden opportunity for me, I was hesitant to make the commitment. But my mother made the decisive difference, urging me to take advantage of the opportunity.

By God's grace, the office was offered to me even though I had not been the first bidder. I was also fortunate that my mother had some beautiful furniture stored away that happened to be just right for the office. After arranging the furniture for me, she took me shopping for some pictures.

But even as all this was happening, I was still unsure about committing to an office in Illinois when my primary office was ninety minutes away in Waukesha, Wisconsin. When you are in private practice, it is difficult to relocate, even to a neighboring state because your name and your business take so much time to establish. What is more, I knew that Highland Park was already teaming with psychiatrists, whereas Waukesha was an underserved area. Consequently, I could not logically see how I was going to build a practice in Highland Park and reduce my practice in Waukesha.

So when my mother and I went into the picture gallery, I asked God to show me a sign that the move was the right thing to do. As we entered the first store, which carried only about a hundred pictures, I was hoping to find my favorite painting—"The Creation," by Michelangelo. The famous original adorns the top of the Sistine Chapel in Italy. I said, "Lord, if I find that picture in this little store, then I will know that this new office is your will for me."

Well it took all of about five minutes for me to go through all the pictures in the store, none of which was what I was looking for. Then, just as we were about to leave, I went up to the register to ask a question and noticed a half dozen large paintings leaning against the side wall. I looked through them as I was waiting to be helped, and the very last picture was an enormous canvas of "The Creation." I could not believe my eyes! Never before had I even seen it in an art gallery, and here it was, larger than life. Not only that, but my mother offered to buy it for me. We later found a beautiful frame for it and the perfect wall in my office on which to hang it. It ended up in a place where my patients would see it no matter where they were seated.

But finding the picture was much more than a sign that I was to open the Highland Park office. The painting itself defined the work that God had asked me to do, which was to let people know that He is reaching out to them with His love.

God's will continues to unfold...

Not surprisingly, I had acquired only a handful of patients in my first two years at the new office. Meanwhile, my practice in Waukesha continued to thrive. So I kept wondering how I was ever going to make the transition to Illinois. I even began to contemplate selling my new office. But just as I was beginning to doubt God's intention for me to have the new office, another psychiatrist in the building told me that he was going to retire and asked me if I would be willing to take over his practice. Although I did not know how I could possibly take on another doctor's practice while at the same time continuing a thriving practice in another state, the offer reaffirmed my belief that opening the new office had been God's will for me. Nonetheless, the situation remained so complicated that all I could do was sit back and wait to see how God was going to make the whole thing work out.

Well contrary to what I expected, I started to have more referrals in Highland Park than in Waukesha. Meanwhile, the doctor who was going to give me his practice decided to postpone his retirement, which gave me the breathing room to gradually transition my practice to Illinois without having to transfer the care of any of my Wisconsin patients. Over the next ten years, the size of my practice in Illinois gradually grew, while my Wisconsin practice slowly dwindled to the point where I was eventually able to leave Wisconsin and continue to see most of the remaining patients in Illinois. Meanwhile, the doctor who was going to give me his practice wound up retiring without sending me very many patients, which was about all that I could accommodate.

To make this whole thing work out, God had to intervene in several ways. He had to prompt me to make the last-minute telephone call about the office space, He had to inspire a colleague to offer me his practice while at the same time keeping him from giving it to me, and He had to direct more new referrals my way in an over-served area where I had not been established than in an underserved area where I had been established. How is that for some divine assistance?

The Finger of God

Late one evening on the way home from work, I had to stop for gas. So I pulled into a gas station, filled my tank, and paid at the pump with my credit card. But about half a mile from the gas station, I noticed that my gas tank was less than two-thirds full. I couldn't understand that because I had pumped over fifty dollars worth of gas. Even at exorbitant gas prices, that had always been enough to fill my tank completely.

Thinking that maybe the pump was broken, I turned around and drove back to the gas station to get the rest of my gas. But when I went in to tell the attendant what had happened, he had an odd look on his face and specifically asked me to wait while he finished up a telephone call. When he had got off the phone, he told me that he had just finished reporting me to the police for failing to pay for my gas. On the counter was a sheet of paper with my license plate number written on it. When I told him I had come back to get the rest of my gas, he said, "Yea, why did you come back?" I told him I had pumped fifty-four dollars worth of gas and on my way home noticed that my tank was only half full. His response was, "That's impossible. You filled your tank with gas and drove off without paying." So I said, "Come on out to my car, and I'll show you."

So we walked out to my car, and I turned on the ignition. To my surprise, the gas gauge went right to full—passed full. Shocked by what I saw, I said, "Let's go in and I'll pay you." As he was swiping my credit card, he told me that all the pumps had recently been serviced and that I must not have swiped my card correctly. He said he assumed that I had just driven off with the gas because that was what a number of people had done in recent days.

On the drive home, I was reviewing what had happened and realized that had I not gone back to the gas station, the police would have come knocking on my door in the middle of the night, and I would have been completely framed by my circumstances. I had no witnesses who saw me pay, I had no receipt, it was late at night, there had been a recent rash of thefts, and my gas tank was full. So had I not rectified the situation while I had the opportunity, I would have found myself facing allegations of theft that could have ruined my professional career.

But what had sent me back to the gas station was the faulty reading on the gas gauge. Because my gas gauge had never done that before, I felt certain that it was the finger of God that held back the gas gauge as a warning that I needed to go back to the gas station.

For the next six months, I checked the fuel gauge reading immediately after filling my tank with gas. On every occasion, it moved to the full position the moment I started the engine, just as it had always done prior to that night. Even if one considers that the fuel gauge phenomenon does occasionally occur in automobiles, the fact that it occurred the one night that I really need it to makes it far more likely to have been an act of divine intervention than a mere coincidence. No less remarkable was the fact that I had interpreted the faulty gauge reading not as a mechanical problem but as a very definite indicator that I had not gotten all the gas I had paid for. Without God's help, I probably would have assumed that the fuel gauge was just slow to register the gas, particularly because I had been so tired that night and just wanted to get home. Then again, there would have been a good chance that I would not have noticed it at all or that I would have noticed it after it had corrected itself. Thus, I believe that God intervened in three ways: first, by holding back the fuel indicator; second, by causing me to take notice of the faulty reading; and third, by influencing the way I interpreted the reading.

With God All Things are Possible

S everal years ago I had gotten into a jam as I was packing up my apartment in Wisconsin on the last day of my lease. Besides the deadline to vacate the apartment, I had to make an early morning flight from Chicago to Phoenix, where my kids would be anxiously awaiting my arrival. Because I was planning to give most of my belongings to charity—what amounted to nearly everything I had accumulated since I had left home for college twenty-five years earlier, I was completely dependent upon the Salvation Army to make their scheduled midday pick-up.

But about an hour before their scheduled arrival, I received a telephone call from the driver telling me that they unfortunately would have to reschedule the pick-up for the following week because one of the movers had twisted his ankle. In a panic, I told the driver that I had to be out of my apartment by midnight and that I would have nowhere to store my things. He apologized for the inconvenience but said there was nothing he could do because his partner had to go to the hospital. Well I was certainly able to understand that because if any of their other pick-ups were like mine, they would need two strong movers, if not three. Nevertheless, I had no leeway; I had to get everything out of the apartment by midnight because my Landlord had already scheduled a new tenant to move in almost immediately. So as hard as it was for me, I politely told the driver that I understood. I then frantically began calling other donation centers, including Good Will and St. Vincent DePaul, but none of them was able to schedule a same-day pick up.

So in a tizzy, I sat down and started to pray, "Oh God, what am I going to do? I promised the kids that I would meet them in Phoenix, and here I am stuck trying to get out of this apartment! Please help me...please find a way." With that, I had the thought that I should again call the Salvation Army and ask if there was any way they could pick up my things. But the operator told me that there was nothing she could do because the mover who had injured himself had to be taken to the emergency room. I ended the call telling the operator that I didn't know what I was going to do. So after I hung up, I sat down and started to pray again, doing my best to believe that God would find a way. I then resumed packing, relying on my faith as best I could.

About twenty minutes later, I received a call from the operator at the Salvation Army telling me that she was going to manage the store, which would free up another mover. She said she couldn't guarantee it, but she was going to try to get a moving van over to my apartment within a few hours.

Well low and behold, about an hour later, two movers from the Salvation Army pulled up to my apartment with the biggest moving truck I had ever seen. Fortunately, the entire thing was empty because my apartment wound up filling the truck from end to end. In fact, it took about twenty minutes just for the movers to force the door of the trailer closed after they had squeezed in the last remaining piece of furniture.

I finished packing the rest of my belongings into my car no sooner than the stroke of midnight. Amazingly, I managed to do so with no more room to spare than that moving truck had had. When I arrived in Phoenix the next morning, I played the first of what would be four consecutive rounds of golf with my son without the slightest ache or pain despite having spent the proceeding thirty-six hours hurriedly packing up all that heavy stuff with no food, no water, no sleep! As it is written: "With God, all things are possible."

Not Dead, Just Passed Away

A dear friend of mine passed away a few years ago. When I arrived at the church for his funeral, the atmosphere was very somber, and some of Dean's family members were weeping in their pews at the front of the church near the open casket.

I immediately took my place in a short procession to pay my respects. But as approached the casket, something very unexpected happened. I started to smile from ear to ear, nearly to the point of laughter. I could not believe that I was doing something so inappropriate. I even worried that Dean's family members might see the grin on my face and be offended.

As I tried to maintain my composure, I began to realize what had happened. Dean had told me a joke! I had actually been experiencing an emotional response to a communication that bypassed my intellect. Absent from the body, Dean was communicating with me spiritually; that is, heart to heart.

As I thought more about it, I began to realize that Dean was being his normal self. Whenever we would get together, he would greet me with a joke. Still, it made me wonder because I have been to many funerals, and nothing like that had ever happened before.

At the conclusion of the church service, each of us approached the casket once again to pay our last respects. As my turn came, I thought to myself, Oh boy, I'll bet Dean is going to tell me another joke. But despite being prepared this time, the experience was a completely somber one. Dean did not say anything to me.

I define this as a miracle because it reminded me that life is everlasting and that death is merely a transition, a passing from this world to the next.

The Power of the Holy Spirit

Last summer I met a woman at the pool who would go for a swim at about the same time as I every evening. Initially, we began talking about how warm the water was and how therapeutic both of us found swimming to be. Then we talked about how many years each of us had been swimming and where. Anyhow, after we had gotten to know each other better, she one day commented that I must really love the water. When I asked her why, she replied, "Because you're so happy when you are here." I said, "No, the reason I am happy all the time is that God has given me the Holy Spirit through faith in Jesus Christ." The look of shock and confusion on her face made me realize that it was no easier for her to hear than it was for me to say, for I had been under the impression that she was Jewish. Anyhow, her response was, "I don't understand." And so I took the opportunity to tell her about how God had sent His only-begotten Son into the world to take our sins upon Himself so that we could be justified in living a new life of joy and abundance. She then asked me if I really believed that. When I assured her that I did, she said she could not understand the meaning of it. She went on to tell me that she had been attending a local Synagogue each week but that it was more for social purposes than for worship. That having been said, I encouraged her to give serious thought to giving her life to Christ so that she could have what I had. She told me that she would like to do that.

When I saw her at the pool the following day, we got to chatting again. The conversation began with some superficial talk; but after a bit, I asked her if she had done it, if she had given her life to Christ. She said she had not because she just could not understand how it works. And so I continued to teach her about the Lord's Gospel.

Though she listened with much intrigue, she explained that she could not understand how a scientist like myself could believe in something so intangible. So I helped her see that there are many things that all of us believe in that are invisible and intangible...love, for instance. She seemed genuinely impressed with my example and could find no grounds upon which to argue the point. And so the discussion continued.

After that day, I made a decision not to bring up the topic again lest she think that I was trying to pressure her. In the days that followed, I continued to see her at the pool, but when we talked, the topic did not come up. About a week later, I decided to pray for God's assistance in my efforts to help her. When we ran into each other at the pool that day, she began by telling me that she still had not given her life to Christ. So we were back to discussing the Gospel. That day was unusual because we were the only ones at the pool. It made the conversation very private until a young man with long black hair and a demeanor that gave me the impression that he was some New Age rocker entered the pool. As he approached us, he could clearly hear everything that I had been telling the woman about salvation and Jesus Christ. My inclination was to quiet down, especially with a guy like this overhearing the conversation. But that faithful evangelist in me, the Holy Spirit, inspired me to keep right on talking as boldly and loudly as I had been before he arrived. When the young man heard what I was saying, something completely unexpected occurred. He spontaneously joined in by asking the woman, "Don't you know that Jesus Christ is the Savior of the world and that you must surrender your life to Him if you want to be saved and live a new life?" Without any comment from me, he went on preaching to her, repeating almost verbatim what I had been telling her during our previous discussions at the pool.

Well needless to say, she was astonished. As she listened to him in amazement, I realized that they had no need of my help, and so I quietly went back to swimming laps. About ten minutes later, I rejoined the conversation to tell the young man that he was an angel sent by God in answer to my prayer that God would help me minister to this woman. He was moved almost to tears and said he found it strange that he even came to the pool that day. The woman then said that she was bewildered by the fact that he and I did not know each other and that the whole thing seemed like a divinely arranged coincidence. Well there was no doubt in my mind that the same spirit—the Holy Spirit—had been at work in all of us!

A Warm Welcome

Several years ago, I attended a local Catholic church near my grandmother's house with the possible intention of attending services there on a regular basis.

Feeling a little shy, I took my seat in the back row. But as we were waiting for the service to begin, one of the ushers laid a hand on my shoulder and asked me if I would help out by carrying the cross up to the altar during the opening procession. The request came as a surprise because I was not even a member there. So I interpreted it as a sign that the Lord was welcoming me into the congregation.

I have been attending services at that church for many years now, and never since that day have I seen the regular ushers need or ask anyone for help.

A Wise Decision

Years ago a relative of mine invited me to make an investment. He had information that led him to believe that any investment I made in the stock would bring me a two to three-fold yield within a year's time. He himself had been investing in that market for some time and had been doing quite well.

Seeing that I had some extra money at the time, I seriously considered his offer. But as I thought about the wisdom of such a venture, the words of St. Catherine of Siena from her masterpiece work *The Dialogue* came to mind, wherein she advised against monetary investments because such activities were at odds with charity and faith in God. Yet I wondered, was her advice outdated? After all, she was writing in the fourteenth century.

So I knelt in prayer and asked God to guide me. After a few quiet moments, I received His answer: "Don't do it." Trusting more in God's small voice than in my logic, I opted out.

Then, on a warm sunny morning about eighteen months later, I received a call from the relative who had made the investment offer. Filled with excitement, he told me that the stock had soared to three times its original value! Between the thrill in his voice and a quick calculation of all the money I had lost by not investing, the round of golf I was headed to play was ruined. I kept kicking myself and asking God why He had given me the wrong advice.

In the days that followed, the pain of my loss caused me to feel a disdain for money. As I was mulling it over in church that Sunday, I decided to take all the money I would have invested and give it to charity.

Then, less than a year later, I received another call from the same person. This time he sounded anxious and depressed as he proceeded to tell me that the stock had crashed, the company was in trouble, and he had lost everything. I felt so sorry for him. All I could do was thank God and St. Catherine for guiding me with their wisdom and love.

An Angelic Vision

Awhile back, I had to make a crucial decision about some charity work that I was involved in. A few days prior to announcing my final decision, I had a dream that warned me about the implications of my continued involvement.

In the dream, I was making a house call to a wealthy patient of mine. As I was leaving the patient's home, I noticed some foam board and large plastic wrappings out by the trash and thought it could be used by some of my homeless patients. I wanted to ask the man and his wife if I could take the stuff, but I really didn't think they would understand. So I quietly threw it into my Landrover, hoping that no one would see me. I then pulled out of the driveway in search of the main road.

Because I was unfamiliar with the area, I was having trouble getting out of the subdivision. Unable to find the main road, I stopped and asked some tree-trimmers for directions. When I rolled down my window, I caught the attention of one of the workers, who was holding some loose branches in his hand. "I saw you take that stuff," he said. "I think you ought to put it back because you did not ask permission to take it." As he spoke, I thought to myself: how does he know I took that stuff? He and his crew are much too far away to have seen me. And why should he care anyway?

Well I could only conclude that he had knowledge and insight beyond the realm of normal human capacity. I also knew that he was justified in telling me to return what I had taken. The problem was that if I pulled back into my patient's driveway to return the stuff, I would likely be seen, and the whole thing would turn into a messy embarrassment. On the other hand, I would remain a thief unless I returned it. As I was debating what to do, I began to realize that my efforts to help the poor had gotten me into a no-win situation.

When I awoke from the dream, I realized that the tree-trimmer was an angel warning me that my continued involvement with the charity would put me in a no-win situation and that I had better get out before it was too late.

Convinced that the dream was a divine revelation, I withdrew my affiliation with the charity while I still had the chance. However, I would never have had the insight and confidence to withdraw if it had not been for the dream. Years later I would learn that my decision had saved my professional career.

An Angel and a Friend

After I moved back to my hometown of Chicago in 1997, I returned to the church in which I was baptized. However, the liturgy and prayers of the Holy Catholic and Apostolic Church of the East are still said in the ancient language of Aramaic. This created a dilemma for me because I wanted to understand what was being said in church without leaving the spirit of the church where I was baptized.

Not knowing what to do, I eventually began to pray that the Lord would give me the ability to understand what the priests were saying. I was not interested in learning the language per se; I just wanted to understand what was being said. Though it was a completely foreign language, I trusted that with God, all things were possible.

About two or three weeks later, a man who I had never met before approached me and introduced himself as I was leaving the church. I politely said, "Hello," and that was the end of it. The following week, the same man approached me again and said his name was Tony. I politely told him my name, and again, that was the end of it. I really had no interest in socializing. After all, I did not speak the language of most of the parishioners, and my chief reason for going to church was to honor God, pray, and receive Holy Communion.

The following week, Tony again approached me as I was leaving church. This time I thought to myself, okay, since this guy keeps coming to talk to me, I am going to ask him to do me a favor. I am going to ask him what the priest said in the sermon.

So when I asked him, he thought about it for a moment and then started to chuckle. "You know," he said, "I really can't tell you; I wasn't prepared for that question. But if you would like, I will pay closer attention next week so that I will be better able to answer your questions."

From that point on, Tony translated what the priest said each week. After a while, he got really good at it. Eventually, he got into the habit of taking notes during the service, after which we would routinely sit down together in the social hall and discuss the sermon.

As time went on, I began to realize that God had answered my prayer. Beyond that, the process was really helping Tony. He told me that it was benefiting him in several ways. It forced him to pay better attention to what the priest was saying, it made him come to church on a regular basis, and it increased his own understanding of the gospel. But the greatest aspect of the miracle was that Tony became my best friend.

In a simple but profoundly loving way, God had done far more than help me understand what the priest was saying; He had sent me an angel and a friend.

Miracles Around the Writing of Images of Heaven

A host of signs and wonders occurred during the writing of my first book Images of Heaven. The large number and spiritual significance of these occurrences, many of which I will discuss here, helped convince me that the book was an inspired work.

That's in contrast to a book I began to write several years earlier, a book that I quickly became convinced was not God's will for me. I had written the first three pages while on an airplane with my five-year-old son. But no sooner had I finished writing the third page than the first two disappeared. That's right, they just disappeared! When my son and I could not find them, I became so frustrated that I began to accuse him of hiding the pages from me. I mean what else could have happened to them? Both of us were strapped into our passenger seats the whole time. When my son insisted that he had not taken them, I put him to the test. I threatened him with severe punishment if he did not return the pages to me. Still, he insisted that he did not have them. When I threatened him again, he looked me straight in the eye and said, "Papa, just forget about it; don't write that book." He said it with such conviction that I interpreted it as a sign that I was not supposed to write the book. So I scrapped the idea and even went so far as to let go of the idea of ever writing a book. I just told myself that we already had enough books and that what was really needed was for more people to read the books we had.

But a short time after the 911 terrorist attacks, I unexpectedly became inspired to write, and to write quickly. Once I got started, I found myself having the passion, the vision, and the energy to devote an enormous amount of time—six hours a day on average—to writing *Images of Heaven*. Over the next five years, I feverishly worked on this book about life, death, and the hereafter with hardly a break. And unlike with the red light that stopped me from writing years earlier, all the lights were green this time. In fact, I felt like the world stood still during the entire time that I was writing the book. The words and ideas often came to me like confetti falling from the sky and popping into my head as quickly as I could write.

In addition to the very definite sense of inspiration that drove me to write the book, there were a number of signs that led me to believe that the book was divinely inspired. For instance, during the time that I was writing the chapter on salvation, I happened to donate blood. When I went into the blood center, I brought along my pen and paper, thinking that I might have some downtime while in the waiting room or even while I was in the chair donating. As it turned out, I did get some writing done in the waiting room. But while I was in the chair donating, with my blood literally flowing into the collection bag, I coincidently found myself writing the section of the book that describes the crucifixion of Jesus, His blood being poured out for humanity. So I thought to myself, what were the chances that I would be writing that particular section when my own blood was being poured out for others?

Another sign that occurred while I was writing that chapter was that I began to notice the sweet smell of lilies in the dusky, austere quarters of my lonely apartment. Though I kept searching for the source of the fragrance, I could not find any. Yet I noticed the sweet smell three nights in a row, and only while I was working on the chapter of the book entitled *Salvation*.

On another occasion, this time while I was visiting the Chapel of St. Joan of Arc for the first time, I quite unintentionally found myself working on the specific section of the book that discusses St. Joan uniting the people of France to defend themselves against the English. As I shared in a previous memoir, everything about that visit was magical.

Later, as I neared the completion of the book, I knew that I had written about ten chapters in all, but I had not yet counted them up. So the thought occurred to me that if this were truly an inspired work, the sum of the chapters would be a holy number, as in the twelve tribes of Israel, the twelve Apostles, or the seven churches in the Book of Revelation. Unfortunately, when I counted up the chapters, the total was thirteen—more unlucky than biblical. Oh well, I thought, what can I do? I cannot now eliminate one chapter just to make the Biblical number, twelve.

Some time after I had accepted the fact that there were thirteen chapters, I was thinking about the chapter I had written on angels. After much debate, I decided to eliminate it because people hold so many different opinions about angels, and I did not want to risk offending anyone unnecessarily. A few days later, I suddenly realized that the book then had twelve chapters!

But perhaps the most convincing sign of God's providence came when I found myself stuck in the twelfth chapter. I had been writing about the return of Jesus Christ, the judgment, and the other events that shall come to pass at the end of the age but did not have enough information to accurately complete the section. So there I sat, stalled at the very end of the book, at the very end of what I believed to have been a five-year-long assignment. Not knowing what else to do, I prayed to God and asked Dr. Lamsa, the world-renowned Bible scholar in whose memory the book was written, to give me the answer.

About a week later, a patient walked into my office and plopped three books down on my desk. She said, "I thought you might be interested in these." I immediately noticed that all three had been written by Dr. Lamsa. I had read all of them, or so I thought. Anyhow, I asked her where she had gotten them because some of his books were out of print. She said she had been at a church book sale and had found them at the bottom of a large bin of books. She had purchased them for five dollars apiece and brought them to me because something told her that I might need them.

Though I already had the books, I thought it would be nice to have extra copies, so I was happy to keep them. After she left, I noticed that one of the books was unfamiliar to me. I was quite surprised because I thought for certain I had read ALL of Dr. Lamsa's books.

That evening after work, I began to read the one book that was new to me. Amazingly, it provided detailed answers to all the questions that had kept me from finishing the last chapter of my book. What a clear answer to my prayer that was! It was one of those rare miracles that are so dramatic and indisputable that the invisible God becomes visible.

I finished writing the book just a few months later, during the early morning hours of resurrection Sunday!

The Importance of the Sabbath Day

In 2005, I completed the first draft of Images of Heaven, the spiritual book that I referenced in the previous memoir. As much as I believe that it was written under the direction of the Holy Spirit, I later discovered that I had made some poor choices along the way, the most important of which was my failure to keep the Sabbath day holy. In my zeal to finish writing the book, I had turned what should have been a six-day-a-week project into a seven-day-a-week one. It is written that a man shall labor six days and do all his work but that he should rest on the seventh. That was something I did not do while I was writing the book because I had turned what should have been for God into something that I thought would make a name for myself.

The Sabbath rest was ordained by God to be a time of prayer, rest, and personal reflection, a time of spiritual refueling in preparation for the week ahead. So while God had richly blessed me for the good work I had been doing six days out of the week, He allowed me to reap the natural consequences of the error I had been making by continuing to write even on Sundays. At the time, a part of me thought that I should have been resting from my work on the Sabbath, but I rationalized what I was doing by telling myself that the book was, after all, about the Bible. Well as time went on, I became so focused on the book that I stopped taking care of myself. I stopped exercising and continued writing even while eating, dressing, and sometimes even driving! Of course, I still went to church on Sundays, but even there my mind was consumed with the book. Little did I know that my academic, albeit Bible-related project was not only hurting me physically, it was also taking me away from God. My thoughts were on God's teaching, but my heart was becoming more and more wrapped up in "my" book.

As I was putting the finishing touches on the book after five years of nonstop writing, I literally went from full speed to doubled over in pain. It was the start of a string of health problems that, by God's providence, have slowed me down, reminded me of the importance of the Sabbath, and led me back to God through a deep inner transformation.

The details of the illness and the way in which it unfolded are miraculous in themselves. Right at the start of a holy period of fasting, I began to experience episodes of flank pain that eventually became accompanied by abdominal distention. I initially thought that I had some kind of virus, but when my symptoms persisted, I began to wonder whether it were something more serious. So I discussed the problem with a colleague but did not have a formal evaluation. As my mother watched me continue to struggle, she started asking me to see a doctor. However, I kept putting off her request, trusting the advice I had received over the phone.

As time went on, I began to lose both weight and strength, and my mother became insistent that I seek a formal evaluation. At the recommendation of a colleague, I had a CAT scan that was read as normal, and so I continued to do little more than discuss my symptoms with colleagues over the telephone. In retrospect, my refusal to have a formal evaluation was indicative of my fear, my pride, my frugality, and my stubbornness. But most of all, it was a display of the selfishness of not considering how my behavior was affecting others, especially my mother, who was becoming paralyzed with fear. By the time I came to my senses and agreed to see a doctor, I had gotten so sick that a simple matter had become a medical crisis.

On formal evaluation, I was quickly diagnosed with kidney stones. I had brought my CAT scan along and told the doctor that the written report had noted two small stones in my left kidney but that there were no obstructing stones. However, when he asked to see the report, it was mysteriously missing. Though I had made a deliberate effort to keep it in the packet of X-rays, it somehow wasn't there. I had the feeling right then that it was lost for a reason. So the doctor said he would ask a colleague to over-read the scan and get back to me with her interpretation. He also recommended some other tests, including an upper endoscopy.

Two days after the endoscopy, he called to tell me that all my test results were normal and that he did not know why I was continuing to feel bloated. Perhaps because such vague complaints are common, he did not recommend any other tests. He just told me to eat well and try to exercise. I was actually disappointed that my test results were normal because I knew that something was wrong.

A few days later, the doctor called to tell me that the radiologist who over-read my CAT scan said that my left ureter had been dilated, suggesting the passage of a kidney stone some time in the recent past but that there were no obstructing stones at the time of the test. However, she had been unable to read the entire scan because the last portion had been cut off. The doctor went on to tell me that it was common to pass stones occasionally, and with no evidence of an obstructing stone, he still could not understand why I was feeling bloated. But the way I reasoned it was that my abdominal symptoms were in all probability related to the kidney stones because they started shortly after I had begun to feel the stones passing. So I wondered whether a stone were still stuck in my ureter, perhaps at the very end where the report had been cut off. Was it possible that the first radiologist either did not see the stone or had failed to report it? So I went to the medical library to research whether an obstructing kidney stone could cause persistent abdominal bloating.

At the hospital library, I began to sift through a large, two-volume text on kidney diseases. After about an hour of searching, I came across a comment at the end of a long section on renal calculi that briefly mentioned that in some cases, persistent obstruction of the ureter by an impacted kidney stone can cause persistent abdominal bloating. It is often misdiagnosed as irritable bowl syndrome (a common ailment for which there is no specific cure), and is found at autopsy in about one percent of the general population. Actually, irritable bowl syndrome is what I thought I had until the doctor told me that he thought I had passed a kidney stone.

With this new information, I called the radiologist who had initially performed and read my scan, praying that if he had made an oversight, he would be honest enough to tell me. He immediately rescanned me and sure enough, the new scan showed a stone stuck at the end of my ureter. The radiologist apologized for not citing it on his original report and did not charge me for the re-scan.

With the new scan in hand, I immediately consulted a urologist, who broke up the stone with lithotripsy ten days later. Shortly after the procedure, tiny fragments of the impacted stone began to pass, and my intestinal function slowly began to return to normal.

By now you might be wondering why I see this horrible experience, including the misreading of my CAT scan, as a miracle. The reason is that the delay in diagnosis allowed me to become sick enough to learn numerous practical and spiritual lessons. On a practical level, I learned that physicians face many potential barriers to treatment when they seek medical care for themselves. These barriers are so numerous, so complex, and in many ways so subtle that I will not even begin to elaborate on them here. What is most important is that I learned them in a way that has inspired me to share what I have learned with the next generation of doctors. It's an issue that was not addressed when I was in medical school, but clearly needs to be addressed. My personal struggle with illness also allowed me to see things from the patient's perspective, something that has increased my effectiveness as a physician in ways that no amount of formal training or clinical experience could have. On a spiritual level, the experience shattered my pride, which allowed me to begin to see how flawed I was as a person. In conjunction with that aspect of the miracle, I came across a book in my office library entitled *Confession: The Forgotten Medicine.* How this book had gotten there is beyond me, and what was equally amazing was that I happened to see it amidst hundreds of other books at a time when I really needed it. Anyhow, as I read it in my weak and humbled state, I was inspired to go to confession for the first time in my life.

Unlike with my physical illness, I sought treatment for my spiritual illness right away. Immediately after reading the book, I set out to find a priest to hear my confession. Not knowing where to go or how to arrange it, I asked God to direct me to a trustworthy priest. Immediately, a certain monastery came to mind, and an inner voice told me to stop what I was doing and go there right away. So I quickly got dressed and drove to the monastery not knowing if a priest was even on sight. Less than an hour later, I was walking into a private room with a priest. It was as if he had been there waiting for me.

When I came out of the room, I felt like a great weight had been lifted off my shoulders, like I had just received a clean bill of health! As I got into my car, I asked the Lord why I had not been so quick to seek medical help when I first doubled over in pain. The answer was simple: spiritual healing is more urgent than physical; and in my case, I had to suffer physical illness in order to recognize the urgency of my spiritual healing.

The night after I went to confession, I had a dream. My sister was behind the wheel of the car, and we were on a towering bridge, about three times the height of the Golden Gate. As she was talking, I felt that she was approaching a turn too quickly, and so I cautioned her to slow down. But the distraction only made things worse, and she lost control of the car. We crashed through the guard-rail, and suddenly we were flying through the air, falling to our deaths. It felt completely real as I saw myself falling hundreds of feet toward the water. Strangely however, I had no fear; having just gone to confession, my soul was completely at ease, and I was prepared to die. The last thing I remembered as my sister and I were falling toward the water was that I was shouting out to her that there was nothing to fear, that we were in God's hands! In psychiatry we say that dreams are often a reflection of our waking thoughts and feelings. This dream was certainly a demonstration of that.

Unfortunately, most of the distressing bloating in my abdomen persisted even after the surgically-shattered kidney stone had passed. Though I thought perhaps I just needed to give it more time, I went back to the medical library to revisit the section of the urological textbook that had helped me diagnose the impacted stone in the first place. Interestingly, I was unable to find it no matter how hard I looked. But in my frustration, I thought to myself: if I can't find something that I know is here, how lucky was I to have found it when I didn't know that it was here? That told me what a miracle it was for me to have found that short, life-saving paragraph in a book that was over a thousand pages long!

Still, the question remained: what was I going to do about the bloating? Well I returned to the urologist who had removed the kidney stone, and after further review, he told me that he could not explain my abdominal symptoms because all my follow-up tests were normal. I subsequently consulted with nearly a dozen urologists and gastroenterologists, and none of them could come up with an explanation for the problem. Even an exhaustive review of the medical literature did not provide a clue. So I again turned to God for help. For reasons unknown to me, I was inspired to pray to the Virgin Mary. At the same time, my mother began to provide reassurance, telling me that God had allowed me to get sick so that I would make positive changes in my life. One of those changes, she said, was to organize my belongings, from my clothes to my professional files. She assured me that by the time I had finished doing that, I would be back to good health.

As I thought about what she said, I estimated that the project would take about three months. Though I had hoped that I would be feeling better in the coming months, I could not understand how organizing my things could help me get there. Yet my mother kept reassuring me that by the time I was done, my stomach would be back to normal. Unable to see the logic behind her directive, I failed to take it seriously. So I instead spent all my free time playing golf despite not feeling up to par.

As it turned out, my symptoms did resolve after about three months despite the fact that I did not do what my mother had asked. So I began to attribute the resolution of my abdominal symptoms to the mere passage of time. I even forgot that I had prayed to the Virgin Mary for help. And what do you know? For no apparent reason, my symptoms began to return. At first I thought it was just a temporary setback; however, I continued to get worse until I was virtually back to where I started.

So I returned to the Virgin Mary in prayer, apologizing for my ingratitude and lack of belief that she had intervened on my behalf. There, on my knees, I again asked for healing. A few weeks later, the bloating once again began to resolve. This time I continued to thank Mary for helping me, remembering her every day for almost a year. During that time, I not only retained my intestinal health, but my stomach actually got flatter than it had been before I got sick!

Just when I was getting to think that all my health problems were behind me, my obedience was again tested. Concerned about my dental health, my mother asked me to switch to her dentist. She had been seeing him for years and really believed in him, so she wanted me to have the same benefits. I reminded her that I had already seen him twice in the past. The first time, he recommended braces, which I followed through with and was grateful for. The second time, he had recommended a filling that I thought was ridiculously over-priced. So I subsequently scheduled an appointment to have the tooth filled by my own dentist. At the appointment, he told me that my mother's dentist wanted to drill the wrong tooth!

So not only was I unwilling to go back to my mother's dentist, I didn't want her to go back to him either. Nonetheless, she continued to urge me to transfer my care to her dentist. We eventually got into an argument about it, and as we were arguing, something deep inside began to tell me that I should not argue and that I should just listen to her, lest something worse than my first illness come upon me.

But I chose to ignore the admonition, just as I had chosen to put off the cleaning and organizing my mother had wanted me to do. Well little did I know, but I already had another medical problem brewing. I was developing an injury that was the result of not giving my body enough time to recover after the kidney stones. You see, I had been laid up for months before the stone had been diagnosed, and after it was removed, I immediately returned to strenuous physical activity despite the fact that I was still dealing with the abdominal symptoms.

I eventually discovered that the injury could have been avoided had I given my body the necessary recovery time, recovery time that I naturally would have had had I obeyed my mother and spent those three months cleaning and organizing. With that in mind, I renewed my efforts to be obedient. I began by reviving the great respect that I had always had for my mother, and I made a conscientious effort to do the organizing that she had told me to do. Surprisingly, I found that simple clean up to be worse than boring; I found it to be down right impossible! You see, every time I attempted to clear the clutter by getting rid of something, I feared that I might someday need that thing. My tendency to hoard quickly made me realize that I had become more attached to things than to God, more reliant on what I owned than on my faith. So the simple assignment my mother had given me had much more profound implications than I realized. In essence, God was telling me, through the voice of my mother, that He was not going to lift my burden of illness until my faith in Him had been revived, and the simple exercise of cleaning my room was part of that revival.

Seeing the mess I was in both physically and spiritually, I again turned to the Virgin Mary. A few weeks later, I suddenly began to realize that I was not sick anymore. Oh I was still having some physical pain, but the perception of being sick had been lifted from me. With that, I also discovered a new-found ability to throw things away. I think I got rid of about two hundred pounds of unneeded papers and old books in a span of only three hours. And what made that possible? Faith. You see, in parting with those things, I found myself gravitating toward God, who is the true source of everything. It also helped me to become less frugal. As I renewed my faith and my vows to God, I began to see my continued physical problem as a forced spiritual retreat. The fact that I could not physically go out and do much created a golden opportunity for me to get back into the word of God and build my faith more than ever before.

Not only that, God had timed the retreat perfectly. In His wisdom, He synchronized it to the time when my grandmother would lose her ability to walk independently and would need more of my time and attention than I would have been willing to give her had I been feeling great and on-the-go. Simultaneously, He worked changes in my medical practice to accommodate my need for down time. For the first time in nearly twenty years, the rate of new referrals began to decline, and many of my most time-consuming patients either became better or went elsewhere for treatment. I was even taken off the hospital call schedule because of an unexpected change in hospital policy. All these miracles have created the opportunity for me to care for my grandmother as well as rekindle my faith by watching inspirational movies with her and spending time in personal reflection and Bible study.

The more I saw myself benefiting from this spiritual retreat, the more I realized that my medical problems were a blessing from God, carefully designed to help me recognize, among other things, the great value that He places on even the simplest acts of obedience. With that in mind, I decided to surprise my mother and transfer my care to her dentist. Given that he was not only over-priced but also wanted to drill the wrong tooth, it was one of the most difficult acts of obedience I had ever undertaken. I felt like I was signing a consent form to be operated on by a surgeon who I knew was going to cut a nerve and leave me in pain for the rest of my life! That made it the single biggest act of faith I had ever contemplated. So for the sake of obedience, I prayed for the strength to put my health in God's hands rather than my logic.

When I went for my appointment, my mother's dentist immediately recommended that I see his new hygienist. She was very nice, and a few minutes after beginning to work on my teeth, she stopped and said that I needed a "deep cleaning." Deep cleaning! I thought. No hygienist had ever recommended that, and I had seen quite a few. But her warmth and genuine concern persuaded me to trust her. She said the cleaning would require four appointments but was necessary for the long-term health of my teeth. She also said that for the procedure, I would require local anesthesia. Well that wasn't too reassuring, so I again began to question what I was getting myself into.

To my surprise, she cleaned my teeth with the utmost gentleness and precision. I did not feel the slightest bit of discomfort either during or after the procedures, even though she had warned me that I would. I later told her that she aught to have been a brain surgeon rather than a dental hygienist, and I really meant it. As she worked on my teeth, it felt more like a message than a cleaning, more like she was painting the Sistine Chapel than cleaning my teeth.

A short time after the cleaning, the cold sensitivity I had been accustomed to disappeared, and so I knew the procedure had been effective. Beyond that, the hygienist inspired me to take meticulous care of my teeth, something that no previous dentist or hygienist had been able to do. Between the skill of the hygienist and the proactive style of my mother's dentist, I eventually came to realize that God had richly blessed me for placing my trust in Him and obeying my mother. What an unexpected turn of events, I thought to myself. It once again affirmed that we can never go wrong by trusting God.

As I look back on all that I have learned through my storm of health problems, I have come to a deep realization that God used the storm to get my attention. In reaching out to Him for a life-raft, I have become aware of how far from Him I had drifted. I had become so rapped up in my work that I stopped keeping the Sabbath, stopped drawing on the word of God. In so doing, I had lost my spiritual compass and had become increasingly selfish, conceited, and competitive in my thinking. The experience has taught me that the word of God is food for the soul and that meditating upon it is a spiritual exercise that must be done on a regular basis in order to avoid losing spiritual strength. The quiet time that my physical limitations naturally created allowed me to correct the many flaws in thinking and behavior that had cropped up like weeds in a lawn that had been neglected, and so I have learned first-hand why God COMMANDED us to keep the Sabbath day holy.

A Message From Above

A few years ago, my elderly grandmother, with whom I live, started telling me that she won't be here much longer and that I should get remarried. I really did not like the idea because, having been married once, I know it would distract me from the work God is calling me to do.

Even if I did meet someone who was willing to make the sacrifice of supporting my career, it would not be fair to her, and I told my grandmother so. Nevertheless, she gradually became more insistent, eventually telling me that she would not rest in her grave unless I promised her that I would remarry if the opportunity presented itself.

After awhile, I started thinking that perhaps God was trying to tell me something through her. So I started to open my heart to the possibility of meeting someone. Just a few days later, I came home in the evening while my grandmother was knitting, and she said, "You know, I keep making mistakes." As she continued to knit, she said, "God talks to me, you know. A little while ago, He told me to stop knitting, but I didn't listen, and now I keep making mistakes."

I have no doubt that God speaks to my grandmother, and so I took the liberty to ask her if He had ever said anything to her about me. "Yea," she said, as she looked up from her work. "Well what did He say?" I asked. She said, "He told me, 'Why do you keep telling this boy to get married? If he gets married, his wife will be cheating on him while he is at work seeing his patients. Just tell him to be clean, be nice (don't argue), and do whatever his mother tells him because he needs her, and one day she is going to need him.'" When I asked her why she didn't tell me that, she said she was going to but had forgotten.

There are three miracles tucked into this story. The first is that my grandmother rarely goes back on anything she says. So for her to admit that she was wrong in telling me to get remarried is the first miracle. The second is that I had the presence of mind to ask her if God had ever told her anything about me. It was a question I had never before asked her, and I asked it at precisely the right time. The third miracle is of course the fact that God had communicated a message to me through her. What is more, God's message made perfect sense because even when I was married, I felt that God had a different plan for my life. Also, I had been asking Him to find me a spiritual guide, and He reminded me that my mother has always been my spiritual guide.

Faith is a Magnet

Two years ago, there was a visiting priest at our church. He seemed to be especially close to God, and I really wanted to ask him to say a prayer for me. But not knowing how to find him after mass, I just went downstairs and had breakfast as I sometimes do.

As I was eating, the person next to me commented about His Holiness, saying that he was very close to God. At that point, I again thought of asking the priest to say a prayer for me but still did not know how I would find him. Very few people in the church speak English, and the priests, especially visiting ones, are usually either inundated by people or nowhere to be found after church.

After I had finished breakfast, I headed out of the church toward my car. Suddenly there he was—His Holiness was in the church parking lot surrounded by a large group of men. He seemed hurried, so I decided not to interrupt him. But just as I was about to get into my car, a small voice inside said, "Just wait for a moment." Though I could not logically see how waiting for a moment could possibly have made any difference, I have learned to trust God's wisdom more than my logic. So rather than getting right into my car, I paused for a moment and then looked back over my shoulder to where the priest had been standing. Suddenly, he was standing all alone! So I walked over to him, introduced myself, and humbly asked him to say a prayer for me. He did so right there and then. It was another sign of how sensitive God is to our good wishes and His desire to bless us.

He Comforted Me in My Time of Need

Of all the medical tests I have seen patients go through in my twenty years in the medical field, the one that frightened me the most from a procedural standpoint was the upper endoscopy because a long rubber tube about the thickness of a garden hose is put down your throat. In fact, my own fear of the test has caused me to save many patients from having it unnecessarily.

Ironically, the first time I ever really got sick, an upper endoscopy was the first test ordered. Of course, I immediately asked God to be with me through it and amazingly, my fear all but disappeared.

But that wasn't all God did for me. When the day of the test arrived and I was in the examining room waiting for the gastroenterologist to come in for the procedure, the nurse asked me what kind of work I did. When she heard that I was a psychiatrist, she immediately started to ask for advice on behalf of a family member. Suddenly, I went from being the patient to being the doctor, and I felt like I was transported to the comfort of my own office.

Just as I finished answering the nurse's questions, the doctor arrived and started the procedure as if he had been interrupting something more important. Thus, in answer to my prayer, the Good Lord did more than comfort me, He allowed me to comfort someone else! A few moments later, I received an injection and the next thing I knew I was in the recovery room resting comfortably.

The Wonder of Trusting God

This Christmas my mother said she thought we should go to church together. Because I was still having so much difficulty walking, I really dreaded the idea. Not only would I be faced with the challenge of finding parking within close walking distance, I would also have to climb the steep staircase up to the church hall. Once there, I would have to remain standing during the service because all the seats were sure to be taken. Nevertheless, I agreed to go.

Just as I was getting ready for church on Christmas Eve, my mother called and said she was afraid that we would not be able to find parking close to the church. And since she could not drive my Landrover, she was afraid that I might get stuck waiting in the car. I agreed with her, and then came a long pause on the telephone as both of us tried to decide what to do. After some debate, my mother said she wanted me to decide.

Although part of me wanted to take the easy road and stay home, a bigger part wanted to demonstrate my gratitude to God for all that He had done and was doing in my life. As I thought about that, I told my mother that we ought to go and see what God was going to do. I reminded her about the parking spot that God had opened up for us right in front the last time we had gone to church together and how He could do it again if He wanted to. If not, I was content to drop her off and just wait in the car.

Well it was a real gamble because Christmas Eve is the busiest night of the year at our church, and finding parking on that night is always far more difficult than any other day. In the preceding twelve years, the closest parking I had found was approximately eight blocks away, and that was after more than half an hour of searching.

When we arrived at the church, voila! There was not one but two parking spots available right in front. But that's only the first part of the miracle. When we went upstairs, the church was, as expected, so packed that there was standing room only. But about five minutes after we arrived, one of the ushers singled out my mother and me from among all those who had been standing, most longer than we had been, and seated us at the front of the church. I had actually been given the very first seat at the foot of the alter!

At the conclusion of the Divine Liturgy, all of us rose to receive Holy Communion, a process that at our church normally takes about an hour because the lines are so long. As usual, I began the long wait to receive Communion. But as I stood there humming along with the choir, I began to notice that people around me were trying to get my attention. Then I saw the chief priest and his Deacons just standing there, waiting for someone to come up for Communion. Suddenly I realized that everyone was waiting for me! Since I had the first seat in the House, I was to be the first among the more than one thousand people to receive Christmas Communion. The thought of being the very first to receive the Lord on such a blessed night was so far from my mind that I could not recognize the honor even when the people around me were prodding me to start the procession. This was God's loving response to my mother's and my reliance upon Him and my extra effort to come to His house even when it was really difficult.

Three Signs That I Will Be Healed

When I first injured myself and saw that there was not going to be a quick fix, I began to ask God to heal me. Shortly thereafter, my efforts to help someone else in need led me into a telephone conversation with a woman in another state who coincidentally had been suffering from depression for many years without effective treatment. In a lengthy telephone conversation, I shared my expertise and gave her my recommendations. She was so grateful that she offered to pay me any amount for all the help and encouragement I had given her. I told her that no payment was necessary, but seeing that the circumstances that led me to her were related to those that led to my injury, I asked her if she would pray that God would heal me. Enthusiastically, she said, "Not only am I going to pray for you, but this very night I am going to ask my whole congregation to pray for you!" That left me with such a good feeling that I went to bed that evening with complete confidence that God would heal me.

Sometime in the middle of the night, the light in the hallway outside my bedroom was turned on. Because I was sleeping on my stomach, I was unable to see who was standing in the doorway, but I could sense that it was someone who loved me very much. That person walked over to my bed and gently laid a hand on my covers over the injured area of my back. When I awoke in the morning, I asked my grandmother if she had come to my room in the night. She said she had not. When I told her what had happened, she immediately said, "It was Jesus." Though my symptoms were still present, I knew that I would be healed in the Lord's good time.

Several months later, God gave me another sign that I would be healed. As I was changing television stations, I paused momentarily when I heard the host of the 700 Club praying. He said, "There is a person listening right now who has a back injury and pain going down his right leg; the Lord wants to heal that." I knew he was talking about me, for what were the chances that I would cross that station right then and that he would perfectly describe my symptoms? I also noticed that he did not say, "Be healed." Instead, he said, "The Lord 'wants' to heal you, implying sometime in the future and perhaps contingent upon something that the Lord wanted me to do first.

Not long after that, I randomly opened the Bible to a verse that said, "Make your path straight, so that the part that is lame will be made whole." That verse perfectly described my condition and was consistent with the message I have been receiving the entire time that I have been plagued with it—that my suffering has been for the purpose of change.

For the next several weeks, every time I opened the Bible, it was to that same section, a section I could not remember ever reading before, and I have read the Bible from cover to cover. But once I had gotten the message, I could no longer find the passage.

A Perfectly-timed Gift

As I explained in a previous memoir, the disabling physical problem that I developed coupled with the unusual lull in my psychiatric practice left me with the opportunity to care for my grandmother and the much needed time for personal reflection.

But after about a year, I had reached the point where I was ready to share what I had learned during my long spiritual retreat. So I began to incorporate some of my new-found wisdom into my book "Images of Heaven." After about three months of editing, I was ready to move on to my next project in preparation for when I get back on my feet. That's when I started to write this book—a project that I had been putting off for years. I reasoned that there could be no better time to recollect all the wonderful miracles in my life than during this trying time, for the book would hopefully be as encouraging to others as to me.

The problem was that I had been unable to sit at the computer, and I quickly found that I could not write while laying on my back. So I tried to dictate the book into a digital recorder, but that turned out to have too many complications.

Then I remembered that my sister had recently given me her old iPhone. Although I was unfamiliar with it's functions, I had once seen a person use the phone to dictate. When I looked into it as a possible means of writing the miracles book without having to sit at my computer, it turned out to be the perfect solution. The book you are now reading was made possible by my sister's gift and God's perfect timing.

God is Great!!!!!!!!!!!!!!!!!!!!!!!!

The problems we face in this life are an often hard-to-accept but necessary part of our preparation for the age to come because they help us grow in patience, faith, and love, and these allow us to see the beauty of Heaven. As it has been said: the stars never shine brighter than on a dark sky. If we allow our trials in this life to help us grow spiritually, the temporary pain we suffer will have eternal value. The miracle I am about to share is an example of this profound truth.

As I explained in a previous memoir, I had been in perfect health until my proverbial plane crashed and burned. The hellish nightmare began with a painful kidney stone that was misdiagnosed and ultimately turned into a protracted illness in which I gradually deteriorated both physically and emotionally. Although the impacted stone was eventually diagnosed and successfully treated, the physical trauma to my urinary system and the prolonged emotional stress I experienced left me with chronic, severe abdominal discomfort and clinical depression. Despite the strong faith that I thought I had in God, I found myself turning bitter and angry at God for allowing me to go through such a hellish nightmare. In the midst of my despair, I found myself regretting some of the sacrifices I had made for God. At the same time, I found myself both pleading and demanding that He restore my health. After several months of this temper tantrum, I heard God tell me to pray to the blessed Virgin Mary. Now I had never before asked anything of God through our blessed Lady, but I straight way began to plead with her to make intercession on my behalf. Not long after that, all my symptoms resolved, and I was healed!

However, not long after I resumed my usual activities, something began to trouble me. It was the immature way I had handled my illness before God. I felt like I had been tested and that I had failed the test when I essentially demanded to be healed. It was as if I were saying, Lord, I am ready to accept your will for me, no matter what it is...unless of course it is something really unpleasant or difficult for me to bear.

Well God must have agreed with me because less than a year later, I was hit with something even more traumatizing and emotionally stressful--a crippling back injury. With it I felt like God was saying, "I'm giving you another chance to show that you accept my will for you no matter what it is."

As I began to suffer all over again, I recalled having previously told God that I was willing to endure any hardship in exchange for the eternal joy that He has prepared for those who love Him. In response, God had given me a vision of what that suffering would be like. I suddenly realized that that vision was precisely what I was in the midst of experiencing. He had also forewarned me about it in a book called "The Dark Night of the Soul" by St. John of the Cross. In it, St. John explains that God purifies the soul by taking a person through a six to seven-year period of unimaginable suffering in which there is a brief remission followed by a second wave of even greater torment. That was exactly what I found happening to me! I found myself in a world of hurt...suffering, frightened, and confused. And not only did I find myself suffering, but there seemed to be no end in sight...no end even possible! Hence, I felt as though my life were over. It was one of those life-changing experiences that bring you face to face with your own mortality, one that you could call a "near-death experience."

So as I lay there on my back, hour after hour, day after day, I began to think about all that I had accomplished and all that I had failed to accomplish. I began to deeply regret every opportunity for love I had not taken advantage of, every bit of caring I had failed to show, every moment of time I had failed to offer a listening ear. But what I regretted most was the time I had missed with my children as they were growing up, time that I could never make up. And I began to cry inside, cry for myself and for my children. I silently begged forgiveness for the missed opportunities and desperately grasped for the quality moments that we did spend together.

In the process, I began to see myself as so small, so weak, so vulnerable. For the first time in my life, I began to see how hard I had labored and how much energy I had wasted trying to stay on top of my game, trying to stay ahead of others. I began to realize how often I had been more interested in winning than in loving, in having the last word than in making peace. I finally began to see myself as the prideful person that I really was, the conceited person that my successes had seduced me into becoming. And I began to think to myself, wow, is my self-image distorted. I felt as though I were finally seeing myself from someone else's perspective, and boy was that an eye-opener! I began to realize that all my "strength" was really just a show of my immaturity. And so I thought to myself, how nice of people to have put up with me for so long just to placate me; or perhaps it was not so nice of them. Suffice to say that my pain was opening my spiritual eyes and having a powerful healing effect. It was a bitter pill but one with the potential to save my soul.

There were times during this horrific ordeal that I felt like I was in a place far worse than Hell, a place so unimaginable horrific that I was actually jealous of those in Hell! And because of my inability to escape, I at times became so angry at God that I found myself on the brink of declaring war against Him for all eternity. But what kept pulling me back was the strength of my relationship with Him--a relationship of love and trust that had been established through all the good that we had previously done together. What's more, I knew I had nowhere else to turn.

Then finally, after years in this arid dessert, this solitary house of horrors, I began to loosen my grip on all that I loved in the world. Seeing that all my earthly hopes and dreams had been irreparably shattered, I became increasingly numb to them and began to turn my attention to the future hope. I began to focus more and more on my relationship with God and the need to work with Him to prepare myself and others for the kingdom to come. Of course God was thinking of me too. I recall one Easter Sunday on which I thought to myself: today is Easter; it's time to stop pitying yourself for a while and be happy for God...it's His most glorious day, the day His only-begotten Son was resurrected from the grave in victory over sin and death! Nonetheless, it was difficult for me to switch from praying to God to giving to God. Yet with great effort, I managed to forget myself and see the day entirely through God's eyes. I did this once at church and again after I returned home. But just as I knelt to pray at home, something very unexpected happened. The Lord Himself suddenly stepped into my consciousness and asked, "What do you want?" Though simple, direct, and soft spoken, His words were daunting, as I felt like He would give me anything I asked. That realization caused me to shrink back and think very carefully about what I really wanted. I even second-guessed my wish to be healed. After a moment of reflection, I said, "Lord, if it is within Your will, allow me to be healed and to regain all my strength." After praying those words, I heard nothing but silence, and I did not feel any better physically, yet I knew that my request was heard.

During my desert experience, The Lord directed me to three books. As previously mentioned, the first explained that for six or seven years, I would suffer in ways so horrific that words could not describe; but after that--oh happy day!!! The sun would rise higher and brighter than ever before. The second book discussed the eternal suffering of the lost and what was required to enter the Kingdom of God. The third explained the importance of humility and how to practice it. I read all three books over and over, though not wanting to believe that I was in for such a long period of suffering.

In my efforts to find relief of my pain and physical limitations, I consulted five primary care doctors, three orthopedic surgeons, twelve chiropractors, four physical therapists, five athletic trainers, three massage therapists, and spent over one hundred hours in physical therapy. Yet the solution to my problem continued to elude me. So round and around I went on this merry-go-round of treatments, knowing the whole time what was going on but not wanting to believe it or accept it.

Then one day in my sixth year of suffering, I found myself in such a crucible of emotional pain that my soul reached out to God more earnestly and with more passion than ever before saying, "Lord, I will accept this pain for the doing of your will, but open a door for me, a very big door." I had not asked for anything specific, just for something to keep me from becoming destructively angry.

The very next day, I came across a website that described my physical symptoms like a textbook. It went on to discuss a theory that was consistent with everything I had learned about neuromuscular physiology in the Department of Kinesiology at UCLA. The concept of NeuroSoma® seemed to solve the riddle that had been paralyzing me for nearly four years and was threatening to hold me captive for the rest of my life. So after reading all the information thoroughly, I contacted Tamsin Stewart, the hostess of the website. After hearing my symptoms, she made some simple recommendations to address the problem of what she called "hypertonic muscle spasm."

The results were astounding! Her simple dos and don'ts with regard to my physical activities and attempts at exercise were actually helping me. Nonetheless, she explained that I would never be able to return to normal functioning without a precise form of neuromuscular reeducation called KANON (Kinetically Activated Nerve Organ Normalization). Developed by Dr. Thomas Griner in the 1970s, this gentle, safe, noninvasive treatment involves recalibrating the resting tension of spastic muscles so as to stop them from causing nerve irritation.

In my efforts to find a KANON practitioner in my area, I came across a number of websites and therapists who were practicing this treatment. As I studied what they were doing in conjunction with what I had learned from Ms. Stewart, it all began to make sense. I began to understand why some things that I previously thought were helping me ended up hurting me and why I kept taking one step forward in my treatment and two steps backward. As I continued to apply the physiologic principles that I learned on the NeuroSoma® website, my body's consistently favorable response confirmed that the theory behind the concept was correct—that I was suffering from chronic muscle spasm. The moment I realized that my problem was completely treatable, I felt the glory of God shine across the sky with a light so bright that it called to mind the words of St. John in that book I read saying, "you will suffer in ways so horrific that words could never describe, but after that, oh happy day!!! The sun will rise higher and brighter than ever before." Though I was rapidly coming to see that my seemingly insurmountable problem was nothing more than a group of muscles locked in spasm, I was also learning that reconditioning those muscles would not necessarily be easy (hence my lack of previous success) and could be done only through a precise form of neuromuscular reeducation.

After a thorough search for a KANON practitioner, I found none anywhere in my area nor even in the entire Midwestern United States. The only practitioners I could find were in Virginia, Arizona, and California. So I thought to myself, well, God has given me the solution to my problem, but seeing that I have to remain in Chicago to care for my grandmother, I guess my time has not yet come, and I will just have to accept that.

But as the miracle continued to unfold, I learned from Ms. Stewart, who teaches KANON myotherapy in Charlottesville, Virginia, that she recalled one student, Ms. Sharon Drewett, who had come from Illinois to learn the technique. She gave me Sharon's contact information though uncertain about her current residence. When initially I could not reach her, it did not look good. But a few days later, Sharon called me back! Not surprisingly, she seemed to understand my problem like a book, and she answered all my questions in a way consistent with what my body had been trying to tell me all along. Now then, when I asked when I could come to see her, she said she was an hour away in Elgin, Illinois but that she preferred to come to me. I thought to myself, What! three days ago I thought the treatment was inaccessible, and now I am being told that the treatment that could save me from Hell was coming to me, to my own house!

You may recall from a previous memoir that shortly after I injured myself, the Lord answered my prayer for healing by visiting me in my room during the night. He had touched the covers over the area of my injury, assuring me that He would heal me in due time. When the therapist told me she would be coming to my own home, I knew that my time had come and that Jesus was returning to my room to heal me through this unique form of therapy.

Not surprisingly, the therapy turned out to be a complete success! The Good Lord had kept His promise. And that did not negate the value of my four-year-long search for a cure. In retrospect, I believe that it was all part of the plan. I believe that God wanted me to experience the various forms of treatment that are out there so that I could see first hand that none of them get to the root of the problem. He wanted me to see how much time people waste on popular yet ineffective treatments and how unnecessary are the risks and expenses of invasive procedures like spinal injections and surgery when the real answer is so simple. In most cases, the real cause of chronic musculoskeletal pain is not the structural abnormality that might be seen on an x-ray or MRI but tight, spastic muscles that are irritating local nerves. What makes it so deceiving is that the classic symptoms, which often include severe pain and altered sensation, don't feel like simple muscle spasm.

Clearly, God had answered my prayer for healing in a way far greater than what I had asked--a way that would allow me to help others. Today I am stronger and healthier than before I got sick, and I am helping others to overcome just as I did. In retrospect, I can see why God inspired me to start writing a book on my treatment even before I had started to get better!

God Knows What You Need

By the time I had finished writing this book, all while laying on my back using the hand-me-down iPhone my sister had given me, my vision was deteriorating. I was learning the hard way that the iPhone was not made to write books on. So I was forced to take a break from looking at that tiny screen despite my need to continue searching the Internet for a solution to my back and leg problem -- a problem that was not only keeping me from sitting at my computer but was also keeping me from living my life!

In the interim, my sister told me that she happened to see a stand that allows you to use a Kindle or an iPad while laying in bed. When she emailed a picture of it to me, I could not believe what I saw. Nothing could have been more ideal for me at the time! So my mother and sister purchased it for me immediately, and within just a few days, I was using the large touch-screen of an iPad, which happened to have been another perfectly-timed hand-me-down from my sister. Not long after that, I discovered NeuroSoma®, which was the crowning miracle of all the miracles in this book!

One could say that the perfect timing of the iPhone, the iPad, and the bed-stand were all just fortunate coincidences, but I am as certain that they were choreographed by God as I am of the two things for which they were used -- my miraculous healing and the writing of this book! Amen.

Rainbow After the Storm

After my wife left in 1997, she took the kids to Kentucky and remarried. There my son had to work on a horse farm, which he disliked but learned a strong work ethic as he labored side by side with Hispanic minorities.

Due to the circumstances, I did not see very much of him for many years, so I began to pray that God would bring him back to me so that we could make up some of the time we lost together. On a regular basis, I would drive to a local church, and from my car in the parking lot, I would gaze at the cross and ask the Lord to bring my Johnny home to me.

One day, after about a year of praying, I heard the Lord say, "I could bring him to you, but he won't listen to what you tell him because he's too stubborn and proud." As I thought about it, I understood what God was saying because I had seen signs of my son's stubbornness. So I said, "Well Lord, I know you have a way of fixing that too." And I continued to pray.

Not long after that, I was awoken very early in the morning by a desperate call from his mother saying that Johnny had been in a fight and that the young man he hit was in critical condition. She told me that in the emergency room, Johnny got scared that he would be arrested and fled from the police. She said he was hiding under a building and was no longer responding to her text messages. So I told her to have him call me.

After a short time, I received a call from Johnny. He told me that the young man he had punched fell to the ground unconscious. So he immediately picked him up, put him in the car, and rushed him to a local hospital. When police in the emergency room started gathering information for their report, Johnny heard his friends accusing him. Fearing that he would be taken to jail and that the medication he was prescribed for panic attacks would be taken away from him, he fled from the police.

After hearing all of this, I calmly reassured Johnny and proceeded to contact the police. I then tried to contact the parents of the young man who had been hospitalized. Of course, the thought of contacting an attorney also crossed my mind, but that would have to wait; I decided that it was more important to promptly do the right things in good faith. Only after that would I turn my attention to my son's defense.

A local police officer who was uninvolved with the case advised me to have Johnny write up his own account of what had happened and turn himself in. I asked Johnny if he would be willing to do that, and after some discussion, he agreed. So I told him that I would help him organize his personal statement after I contacted the young man's parents at the hospital.

When I tried to contact them, I learned that their son had been airlifted to another hospital where he was undergoing emergency brain surgery. The young man's mother answered the phone but was too upset to talk. She handed the phone to her husband, who told me the doctors feared that their son might not make it. As I apologized, I myself wept, imagining how I would feel if I were the parent and *my* son were the one fighting for his life. Fortunately, I had contacted the young man's parents right away because shortly thereafter we received notice that we would no longer be able to talk to the family or even make any inquiries with the hospital.

Johnny and I then proceeded to work on his personal statement describing what had happened in the incident. When that was done, I advised him to call the police unit that was involved in the case and turn himself in.

As expected, he was placed under arrest and put in jail. When the attorney who my in-laws hired (one of the best in the state) learned that I had advised Johnny to turn himself in with the signed personal statement, he told Johnny that that was the worst advise he could have gotten because the confession made it impossible to defend him. Subsequently, he asked him not to talk to me until the case was over.

As all of this was unfolding, I began to ask God what was happening. The drama of the whole thing was something out of a movie, and the fact that I could no longer talk to my son made me feel as though God was doing just the opposite of what I had been praying for. Worse yet, Johnny was restricted from talking to me at a time when he needed me most!

In spite of it all (or shall I say because of it all) I knew that God was up to something because the timing and magnitude of what was happening were just too extreme to be anything other than God's hand in my son's life. As if the Holy Spirit were speaking through him, Johnny's last words to me before I lost contact with him were, "Papa, I've been humbled."

As I thought about it, I realized that the events leading up to the fight had created the perfect storm to teach Johnny humility and obedience. In the months leading up to the incident, I had been warning him not to spend time with kids who drink and party. But he rebelled against that, saying that my advise was too restrictive. He even went so far as to rebel against the religious aspect of my teaching, saying that he wasn't sure if he even believed in the Bible and Christianity. Thinking that he was invincible, he proceeded to do what he wanted. Using his own logic, he thought that if he himself did not drink, he could safely hang out with those who did. Little did he know that obedience trumps logic: the Bible says, "Honor your mother and your father so that you may live long in the land that the Lord your God is giving you" (Ephesians 6:2). Before the incident, Johnny told me that God's rules were too restrictive. After the incident, his attorney told him that he was not permitted to do anything but go to school and return home. By disobeying God, Johnny had lost more freedom than he would have lost by obeying Him through me. He was also humbled by having landed himself in a no-win situation. You see, what led to the incident was a fight between two girls that Johnny merely tried to break up. It was a no-win situation because on the one hand was the danger of getting involved and on the other was the negligence of doing nothing to help. So he had to make a tough choice. When he elected to break up the fight, he was drawn into another fight, which led to the regretted assault.

As God would have it, the young man's surgery was a success. He had a strong recovery, and Johnny learned that obedience was more important than intelligence. The painful experience also pointed Johnny in the direction of a new and exciting future--the field of law. Johnny said that his hellish experience had given him compassion for all the innocent minorities who are falsely accused and unfairly sentenced because they are not fortunate enough to have the kind of legal representation he had. In sharing his passion to become an attorney, he said that he wanted to study in California and apply to law school at the university I graduated from. In my excitement about this, I told him I would take him to Los Angeles so that we could visit the UCLA campus together. However, the trip never materialized; God had other plans.

As he was preparing to send out his law school applications, I recommended that he share his painful character-building experience in his personal statement to each school. After all, it *was* that experience that made him decide to apply. I told him that his personal statement was so strong that he would likely be accepted anywhere he applied. With that, I advised him to send applications to the top schools in the country, most of which were far away from where I live.

In my efforts to help Johnny get into a prestigious law school, I forgot that I had been asking God to bring him close to me in Chicago. But God did not forget; Johnny wound up being accepted to a school just a stone's through away--Marquette University in Milwaukee, Wisconsin! He later learned that he had the lowest combination of grades and test scores of all the applicants who were accepted to law school this year. Clearly, his personal statement made the difference, and what made his personal statement was his honesty and perseverance in the face of the character-building trial God had walked him through. On the test that really mattered, he did very well, and God rewarded him accordingly.

In retrospect, God had given me far more than what I asked. More than bring Johnny back to me, he taught him the humility and obedience that would make it possible for me to be a father to him. He also gave Johnny *his* wish by opening the door to another school I graduated from, by God's grace a Jesuit school, which would bring him back to his roots in Christianity. Beyond that, He gave him a career in which he could help others through what he had learned!

What is the lesson in this story? That God sometimes answers our prayers with a storm, but you can count on a rainbow if you have faith.

The church parking lot where I prayed.

Christt With Us

I teach Sunday School at church, and one Sunday I decided to ask the class a question. I said, what would you think if I told you I met a man whose father was very wealthy, and because he was tired of life in this corrupt world, he had decided to build a beautiful community on an uninhibited island, a city free of lying, stealing, and cheating. His planned utopia will have clean streets, beautiful homes, and beautiful schools, and it will be a community free of the need for locked doors, police, or even money because everyone will freely share their talents and resources with their neighbors. The man also told me that anyone interested in living there would have to prepare by carefully reading and living by a code of ethics that the father himself had prepared.

No sooner had I finished telling the story then one of the students in the class raised his hand and said, I know, the rich man is God, His son is Jesus, the island is Heaven, and the rules are the Bible. "Very good!," I said. Immediately, another hand went up. Dr. Michael, Dr. Michael, can I read something? Go ahead, I answered.

This is what she read: "Don't let your heart be troubled. Believe in God. Believe also in me. In my father's house are many homes. If it weren't so, I would have told you. I am going to prepare a place for you. If I go and prepare a place for you, I will come again, and will receive you to myself; that where I am you may be also" (John 14:1-3).

Stunned by the appropriateness of the Bible reference, I asked, "Where did you find that?" "I didn't," she replied, "it just popped up on my cell phone while you were telling the story."

The whole class went silent, as everyone knew that she had not had time to look up this reference even if she had known exactly where in the Bible it was. I personally have read the Bible from cover to cover, and I myself would have needed time and a concordance to find it!

As all of us marveled, I said, You see class, the Lord is right here with us; and He is telling us that that's exactly how it is, that His Father is building and that we who want to live there should be preparing every day by studying and living by the words of the Bible.

A Sign of Affirmation

Since the time that I completed the first edition of this book, I have been carrying copies with me in my car in the event that I find someone who I think would be inspired by it. Anyhow, as I was about to get out of my car to go for a swim one day, a small voice inside told me to bring a copy along with me. That's strange, I thought, I'm just going for a swim, so what sense would it make to bring the book with me? But then I wondered, where could such a senseless idea have come from? Well I knew it hadn't come from me, so I could only conclude that it must have come from above. I just figured that God must have had some good reason for telling me to bring the book with me. So I did.

As expected, there was no one to give the book to on my way to the pool. In fact, there wasn't even anyone in the locker room. So I tossed the book into my locker, changed, and went to swim. Well as I was taking a break on the side of the pool, one of the lifeguards, a nice young man who I had been getting to know, deliberately walked over to tell me that he had been summoned for jury duty. He said he was going to purchase a book so that he would have something to do with his down time in the courthouse. Seeing that he had no particular book in mind, I offered him the one in my locker. "What's it called," he asked. "Miracles," I said, "And one of them is that I actually have the book with me!" I then proceeded to tell him how an inner voice had told me to bring the book with me for no apparent reason. I then told him that I suspected he was going to have a lot of reading time the next few days.

A week passed before I saw him at the pool again, and sure enough, he did have to spend a lot of time in the courthouse. He said they had him sitting on standby most of the week. With all the down time, he had managed to get through a reasonable portion of the book despite the fact that, as he put it, he was "not much of a reader."

But that's only the first part of the miracle. When he asked me if I wanted the book back, I suggested that he just leave it on the table in the lifeguard room for anyone else who might be interested in reading it. Well I had no sooner finished telling him that when another lifeguard, a young woman who had been sitting so far away that I am surprised she was able to hear us talking, shouted out, "What book are you guys talking about...is it inspirational?" Before I could answer, the lifeguard with the book started telling her what it was about. Twenty minutes later, that other lifeguard walked up to me as I was resting on the side of the pool and exclaimed, "I'm really excited to read your book!" I took it as a sign that God had accepted what I have written in this book and that He would like others to read it.

+ + +

CLOSING COMMENT

The miracles I have shared in this book were chosen because of their inspirational value and simplicity. There are other miracles I have experienced—some even more wondrous than these—that I have nevertheless omitted either because the details were too elaborate or the circumstances too deeply personal to share.

But regardless of how mundane or inspiring, subtle or dramatic a miracle might sound to some, what is most important is the relevance it has to the individual who experiences it because that is what draws him or her closer to God. The greatest miracle of all is that EVERYONE can live a miracle-filled life. We need only accept God's free gift—Jesus Christ—into our heart, and the divine life begins!

While there are many different religions, attitudes, and beliefs, there is only one story of redemption. Yet the story is so familiar to most of us that it is easy to lose sight of its eternal significance. Because all of us have sinned, all of us had been separated from God. What that means is that none of was able to approach God as our Father in heaven because our sins stood in the way.

But out of His great love for us, God the Father sent His Only-begotten Son into the world to take upon Himself the just punishment for our sins. What God asks of us in return is that we commit ourselves to becoming followers of Christ. Surrendering our lives to Christ is what guarantees our salvation and opens the door to a new life in the kingdom of God. It is the way in which we tell our Heavenly Father that we accept His invitation to become a citizen of the eternal place of rest that He is preparing for those who love Him.

In actuality, we do not ascend to the kingdom when we surrender our lives to Christ but rather God's kingdom descends to us by the power of the Holy Spirit. Once we receive the Holy Spirit, we are able to begin to live the magical life of love that characterizes life in heaven. In essence, God helps us spend the rest of our earthly life practicing heavenly life.

In heaven, there is no need to worry about anything because everything we need is readily available. The same applies to all those on earth who are practicing heavenly behavior in Christ Jesus. Though we are not yet physically in heaven, God blesses us with all the benefits of heaven. Unfortunately, most people are not surrendered to Christ and so are caught in a vicious cycle: they cannot behave like they are in heaven, so they cannot receive the blessings of heaven. This in turn reinforces their carnal behavior and lack of faith, and the cycle continues.

I can say from experience that to the extent that I have lived my life in Christ and conducted myself as if I were in heaven, God has freely given me the things of heaven. This has reinforced my faith and drawn me closer to God; and the closer I draw to God, the closer I am to His next miracle.

Miracles are the evidence of God's favor toward His children. But we must remember that because God loves us, He is more interested in leading us to spiritual peace and happiness—that is, heaven—than in giving us everything we want when we want it. Therefore, if God delays in answering a prayer of a believer, it is not necessarily because He is opposed to it. Most often He merely wants to prepare the way by cultivating in us the love, patience, and gratitude that will allow us to truly enjoy and keep that for which we ask. In order to accomplish this sublime transformation, He asks us to stand firm in our faith even if we have to wait and even if everything in us and around us is telling us to give up. Those who prevail will see their every dream come true!

ABOUT THE AUTHOR

Michael R. Binder, M.D., was born in Chicago, Illinois. He was raised in a home where God was a part of his daily life and where he learned to pray at an early age. From his childhood, he was drawn to the Scriptures, learning to read from a children's Bible and finding inspiration in the lives of the saints.

At the age of eighteen, he began premedical studies at the University of California, Los Angeles. By divine providence, he met Drs. Michael and Kathleen McCann, two university professors who lovingly nurtured his study of medicine and spirituality. In addition to his premedical studies, Dr. Binder served as a lay minister at the UCLA Medical Center.

In 1984 he graduated from the University of California and began medical school at Creighton University, where, in addition to his medical studies, he continued to serve as a lay minister. In 1988 he received his doctorate in medicine from the University of Chicago, Pritzker School of Medicine. From there he went on to specialize in the field of psychiatry, through which he deepened his understanding of the relationship between the mind, the body, and the spirit.

Since 1992 Dr. Binder has dedicated himself to the full-time practice of psychiatry. Though he was able to successfully treat many of his patients, there were some who could not be healed. Unwilling to give up on his treatment-resistant patients, Dr. Binder was inspired to reach beyond the scope of science and medicine. He began to pray for his patients and ask God to help him better understand the mystery of healing. The Lord answered his prayers by calling him back to the Bible, a calling that has allowed him to become a better physician with the help of the Divine Physician—Jesus Christ.

Other books by Michael R. Binder, M.D.

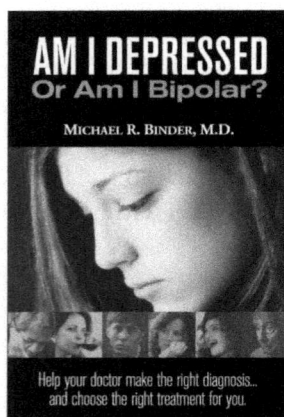

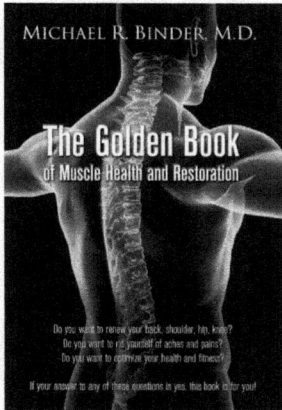

The Golden Book of Muscle Health and Restoration

The Golden Book is a revolutionary look at the hidden cause of chronic musculoskeletal pain and the only effective way to treat it.

Based on his own struggles with chronic pain and the brilliant work of Dr. Thomas Griner, Dr. Michael Binder addresses the little-known but extremely common problem of *hypertonic muscle spasm*. In this life-changing book, you will discover how hypertonic spasm develops, how it causes symptoms, and if you are already suffering from it's ill effects, what to do to get out of pain and stay out of pain without the need of drugs, injections, or surgery. We're talking about truths that are destined to revolutionize orthopedic medicine, physical rehabilitation, and the fitness world! So if you want to preserve the vitality of your muscles and get the most out of them; or, conversely, if you have ever thrown out your back, developed chronic pain in a joint, or experienced frightening symptoms like numbness, tingling, or pain down an arm or leg, this book is for you! Available at www.barnesandnoble.com and www.amazon.com

www.ingramcontent.com/pod-product-compliance
Lightning Source LLC
Chambersburg PA
CBHW052045090426

42739CB00010B/2051